D0847922

They Cry, Too!

ALSO BY LUCILLE LAVENDER

Struggles of a Sinner-Saint

They Cry, Too!

What You Always Wanted to Know about Your Minister but Didn't Know Whom to Ask

LUCILLE LAVENDER

HAWTHORN BOOKS, INC.
W. Clement Stone, Publisher
NEW YORK

to
my man sent from God,
whose name is
John,
pastor to many,
husband to me

Contents

Preface

Ministers are people, too, I think. Ministers are made very special by their Maker, who issues them their special call.

They come in varied shapes and sizes like anyone else but, according to most people, they have a special look. I don't know what it is, but I think this is so because often people exude such surprise: "You don't *look* like a minister!"

They have outstanding talents in every conceivable field of endeavor imaginable. Administration, writing, public speaking, diplomacy, psychology, economics, medicine, good bedside manners, building, maintenance, teaching, counseling, comforting, conciliating, coordinating, and creating.

Ministers have anatomical characteristics that others don't have. They are built not to wear out as easily as normal creatures. They are more resistant to sleep and relaxation, so they can work a sixteen-hour-a-day, seven-day week. And, if they are wakened in the middle of the night by the telephone and they can't get back to sleep, they work on Sunday's sermon.

There is something unusual about their flesh, too. Their skin is extra thick and tough, so they can be roasted for dinner with a minimum of discomfort. And this helps them withstand possessive, particular, and peeved people.

Under this thick skin is a special cushion of insulation that keeps them immune to feelings other earth people have—like never getting angry, despondent, disgusted, or discouraged. It also insulates them against needing love, acceptance, praise, encouragement, and raises in salary.

Ministers are also all-knowing, all-wise, all-comforting, all-controlled, all-put-together and all-ways there.

Do you know any ministers like that? *I* don't! And I ought to know . . . I live with one.

Acknowledgments

This book began with my early childhood memory of a young pastor in a midwestern town, the Reverend B. W. Krentz, who has long since gone to a more beautiful world. He loved children, and I adored him. Even then, I knew instinctively about and empathized with his burdens and his joys.

Though I did not intend to become involved in the ministry, my compassion for ministers grew. Later, in a traveling music ministry, this appreciation and respect for the nature and scope of their service became a personal passion, which still persists.

To all who shared their hurts, their happinesses, their abiding friendships, I am deeply grateful. They *are* this book!

To some special friends who became my mentors, and who would not let me give up—Marieta, Max, and Vera—my love. To Myron L. Boardman for his encouragement; to Judy McKnight, who typed the manuscript; and to Mary Collup, who, for one high-pressure week before the publisher's deadline, sacrificed work and family to help revise, retype, and copy the final manuscript; to the many clergy and lay people who responded to my surveys; to my family who helped us all survive—my gratitude.

Finally, those who read this book and become more understanding of their "man sent by God" will be *my* reward!

They Cry, Too!

1

Why You Should Ask

A real estate salesman, after the sale of a home, reported back to his office with the good news.

"Which house?" asked his fellow employees.

"One of the smaller homes on the edge of the country club district."

"Who bought it?" asked a spokesman for the eager group.

"A minister," replied the salesman.

In flabbergasted unison the staff cried, "A minister? In the country club district?"

A high school student, along with a number of other students, was late for an early morning class. This particular young man was singled out by the teacher.

"Why are you late, Jim? After all, look who your father is!"

The student was a minister's son. Fortunately, he had a healthy attitude and a sense of humor. He grinned as he said, "My father? He's late sometimes, too."

A grammar school student was reprimanded by his teacher for calling another child a liar.

"*You* shouldn't say things like that. Your father is a minister!" she broadcast, loudly enough for the entire class to hear.

THEY CRY, TOO!

When she turned her back to write on the board, there was a noisy thud as a pencil bounced off that child's head, missed an eye, and dropped to the floor. The other children confirmed that another child had, indeed, taken a pencil, denied it, and thrown it when the teacher's back was turned. Neither the teacher nor the child who took the pencil and lied apologized.

A young man, independently wealthy, dedicated his life to the ministry, went to a seminary, was ordained, and pastored a number of fine churches. His parishes were, for the most part, uncomfortable about his financial independence. After twenty years in the ministry he felt he no longer should "subject himself and his family to the gaff," as he stated it. Today he is a leading layman in his church and an understanding friend to his pastor.

Then there was the dear lady who, upon hearing that her pastor and his wife were adopting a child, said, "Now, that's the way I like to think of my pastor!"

All this is to say that lay people and clergy have both been rendered less effective because of the role the pastor, like an actor, is supposed to play, though only rarely does he himself choose it. Usually it is forced upon him by people who place him on a pedestal because they choose to suppose he lives the way they think *they* should. There is a subconscious, sometimes neurotic, need to feel that somebody in town has it all together even though they don't.

The tragedy of the pedestal complex is that it leads to the establishment of one standard for ministers and another for laity, and to discrimination, as in the true incidents presented above. There are some things in life acceptable for lay people, such as accumulating wealth, becoming successful, displaying anger, liking sex, and talking, not so nicely, about other Christians. But these are not acceptable for the clergy, even when society is freeing every other minority!

This must change as we face some of the most exciting days ahead for the Body of Christ—his church!

U.S. News & World Report stated:

> After years of turmoil and declining membership,
> many of America's "main line" Protestant churches
> feel they are on the brink of a revival. The reason: a
> general religious stirring in the nation that not only
> has spurred the dramatic rise of "Jesus freaks" and
> exotic cults but is making itself felt in the more
> traditional churches as well.
>
> "There's no doubt we're going to have a spiritual
> revival, and I think the establishment churches will
> have a big part in it," says Dr. John W. Meister.[1]

The church has stubbornly survived centuries of change,
erosion, attack, undergrounding, persecution, and, of late,
"God is dead" and anti-institutionalism. Miraculously, it
continues to countenance something far more debilitating
than outside pressure. It is the inside indifference of its own
professed adherents—the indifference to the church and to
God's man, through whom he is trying to work in that church.
Yet many of these people can state without hesitation what
they expect from the pastor—for themselves and in his job.
Conversely, these same members rarely think about what the
pastor might expect from them, in their relationship to him
and to the Body of Christ—their church.

In the how-to syndrome of the seventies there are tons of
printed material telling us how to do everything possible. In
religious literature one can learn how to be Christian without
religion, how to receive the Holy Spirit, how to speak in
tongues, how to pray, how to be Christian parents, how to
teach children about sex, how to be Christian in show
business, how to be a Christian husband or wife, how to
witness, and how to form study groups. The list is endless.

A pastor gets his share, too, on how to be an effective administrator, how to be a good pastor, how to organize his church, how to use his time efficiently, how to be a better preacher, how to counsel, how to relate to teen-agers, how to help the elderly, how to build a better church, how to take care of all his people's needs, and how to be responsible in the pulpit. All these well-meaning in-one-easy-lesson suggestions, added to his infinite list·of duties, increase his layers of anxiety, inadequacy, and guilt. They cause him to wonder: "Now what else am I doing, or not doing, or doing wrong?" This author has looked in vain for a book about how to discover and fulfill the needs of the pastor. This unawareness of his needs, indicated by the lack of literature on the subject, may not be intentional—it simply may have been overlooked.

If this handbook is a plea for anything, it is a plea to put aside the artificial differences imposed upon a minister—and his wife. They must be freed from the bondage of generations of man-made notions dictating who they are and what they should or should not do in virtually every area of their lives.

These couples sent by God must also change some of their own antiquated attitudes. They must learn to apply to them-selves what they compassionately have been trying to teach others. Though easier said than done, they must learn to *accept themselves*—their own humanness, their own needs, their own strengths and weaknesses—and come to grips with their own impossible expectations of themselves. They must acknowledge their own limitations, and that they will *never* be able to do and be everything that is expected of them by those they serve. Most of all, they need to know that the world's, i.e. people's, expectations, *are not God's.*

And the people of God must understand that, while they and their pastor have different functions within the Body, they are all called to the same commitment, behavior, and ministry. (1 Cor. 12)

This book is not an overnight happenstance. It is the result of life, lives, living; people, pastors, and churches; and the bringing together of their combined experiences. It involved ten years in a traveling ministry, getting to know well—often intimately—hundreds of pastors and thousands of lay people. Two years were spent in the compilation of data from books, articles, interviews, and surveys. Over a year was spent in writing. The surveys and interviews taken were from clergymen and women, ministers' wives, lay people, church members, the unchurched, psychologists, seminary students, and professors. The percentage of response from a clerical survey sent to forty leaders of religious bodies of the three major faiths of our country was exceptional.

Ninety-two percent returned the long questionnaire thoughtfully filled out. Their motivation for taking time out of busy schedules to personally fill out the forms seemed to be one of deep concern for building a better bridge of understanding between pastor and people. The survey revealed that our national religious life reflects an unusually great degree of restlessness within the clergy itself. The average length of time a pastor spends in a given parish is three to five years. A study at a seminary in Illinois indicates that this short-term pastorate is not as effective as it could be in virtually all areas of pastoral responsibilities.[2] It takes at least that long to get to know the constituents and the community.

Could it be that this gap between laity and clergy is due, in large measure, to a lack of concern, courtesy, etiquette, i.e., good old-fashioned manners on the part of lay people? Is this one of the major reasons for the pastors' constant movement from church to church? It is generally known that 20 percent of the American population moves each year. Traditionally, pastors have transferred more often than those in other professions. There are several hundred thousand pastors serving parishes in the United States. A conservative estimate is that 25 percent move annually, or well over a hundred pastors a day. Some religious leaders believe that one-third would be a more accurate figure—or nearly two hundred pastors moving every day of every year!

These are but a few of the reasons why you should ask about your minister. There is a need to reveal the burdens, pressures, and awesome responsibilities he faces, and people ought to know about them. The following pages will attempt to engender a new awareness and sensitivity toward those the clergy serve. There are suggestions at the end of each chapter to which the reader might like to respond. Some may be checked for personal consideration.

This book is not intended to be theological, theoretical, or otherworldly. It is intended to be candid, practical, and down where-it's-at. Hopefully it will bring people and pastor more closely together in a shared pilgrimage. And some day we may all be presented, a bit more "faultless before the presence of his glory with exceeding joy." (Jude 1:24 AV)

2
Questions about
HIS CALL

A year ago my husband and I attended the memorial service of a close and loyal friend of many years. He had been a pastor of a number of churches throughout his lifetime. His had been a ministry of solid, steady, and loving service, and he was truly "a man sent by God." He grew with the challenges of each church's needs, and as he led his people in spiritual growth, he himself became a spiritual giant.

He did not make loud noises. He was a quiet man, with a keen sense of humor. His calm manner belied a disarming personality and a depth of maturity, which one discovered anew each time there was an opportunity to be with him. He was a loving father and husband, who gave all he had to his Lord, his church, and his family. For those of us who knew him intimately, this is not empty eulogy, this is fact.

However, he, too, had had his share of pain and heartache, which hurt more than the illness that eventually took him. Some disturbing things happened in one of his pastorates. Instead of going to him to help eliminate a problem in its early stages, church members stood by and watched. There were the resultant heartaches in the divisiveness of a staff member and a couple who were among the pastor's closest friends. Our friend refused to let his pain stand in the way of a continuing, caring, Spirit-motivated ministry. Even when most of these misguided people found they had deeply wronged their friend and pastor, they made no attempt to seek reconciliation and forgiveness, though he longed for it, for their healing as much as for his. It never came, though he continued to minister to them in love.

But the experience took its toll. His wife began to see a noticeable change in him during the several years that followed. Those who were involved in one way or another could not help but feel his forgiveness, but those who should have asked for it did not. He pushed this deep within himself and tried not to notice.

Later, he received a call to another church, but not before he had carried his former pastorate on to its highest performance. He and his wife found themselves abundantly happy in their new church, and it proved to be one of their most significant ministries.

He was not, however, a well man. Within two years his health declined drastically. He became critically ill. Surgery was attempted, but he died a few hours later. The neurosurgeon who performed the surgery confirmed the wife's secret suspicions. Yes, he said, it was true that the trauma he had suffered and sublimated, rather than brought out and dealt with, could have been the origin of his illness.

As I looked at this man, our close friend, this body in the coffin, it was not the man I had known. Though he was sixty, he looked eighty. I thought of his great spirit, of his marvelous boisterous laugh, and of some of the hurts he had allowed himself to share with us, and I wept! The church was packed at his memorial service, and many stood to pay homage to this man sent by God. People from all of his pastorates attended.

Later I asked his wife if the friends who had betrayed him and caused such heartache were in attendance. "Yes," she answered emptily, "they sent roses." The silence that ensued screamed out: "Five years too late." How this man had waited for those roses. Roses of a renewed friendship, a revitalized love, or a thoughtful act. Roses of life that would bring happiness and joy. Not roses that were cut, like a severed relationship, to wither and die on a casket.

When God calls someone into the ministry, he does not promise a bed of roses. But if Christian people would try to understand more fully what such a call involved, many of the thorns could be removed. This book addresses itself to those who have a faith, whether they are Christian, believer, church member, or communicant. They all have access to a minister, a pastor, a rabbi, a priest—a shepherd to whom is assigned the growth of the spirit. Each of these believers is sending roses to his shepherd. They may be overt evidences of spiritual growth; involvement and work in their church; kindly deeds; beautiful, blossoming, fragrant roses. Others, instead, send thorns, through their various kinds of negative responses. Far too many send dead, wilted, withered bouquets of complete indifference—far removed from the teachings of the Lord they once professed to know and to his church. They are as dead as the roses they send.

A pastor, regarded as highly successful in a huge metropolitan church, astonished his congregation when he stood to preach. As he approached the pulpit, he reached into his pocket and pulled out a folded letter. He held it up for all to see and explained that it was a letter of resignation that he had been carrying for three years. He was frustrated at having to waste his limited energies and time on trivialities far different from what he believed his ministry ought to be. He was defeated and discouraged when he saw no sign of growth in those he had tried to guide into spiritual maturity. "But" he continued, "if it weren't for the 'Jonathans' I would have read it long ago." A church of thousands sending roses of indifference. He stayed for the few who bloomed, as did Jonathan's love for David.

Our Lord and the Apostle Paul made it clear that everyone is called into certain professions and careers according to his abilities:

> For it will be as when a man going on a journey called his servants and entrusted to them his proper-ty . . . to each according to his ability. (Matt. 25:14, 15 RSV)

> God has given each of you some special abilities; be sure to use them to help each other, passing on to others God's many kinds of blessings. Are you called to preach? Then preach as though God himself were speaking through you. Are you called to help others? Do it with all the strength and energy that God supplies, so that God will be glorified through Jesus Christ. (1 Pet. 4:10, 11 LB)

> Usually a person should keep on with the work he was doing when God called him. Are you a slave? . . . If the Lord calls you, and you are a slave, remember that Christ has set you free from the awful power of sin; and if he has called you and you are free, remember that you are now a slave of Christ. . . . So, dear brothers, whatever situation a person is in when he becomes a Christian, let him stay there, for now the Lord is there to help him. (1 Cor. 7:20–22, 24 LB)

There is no question but that every call, according to the abilities he has given us, is a worthy call if we do it to his highest and our best. Paul must have thought about slaves with the heart of an Abe Lincoln, because he addresses himself to their plight and pleads for kindness from their masters. If he were writing to the churches today, he might have said, "If you are a physician, if you are a carpenter, if you are a contractor, if you are an engineer, if you are a mother, if you are a domestic, if you are an astronaut, if you are a secretary, if you are a president:

> You are now a slave of Christ! You have been bought and paid for by Christ, so you belong to him—be free now from all these earthly prides and fears. (1 Cor. 7:22, 23 LB)

Whatever your calling, whether high or low on the totem pole, you are to do it to the best of your particular gifts and abilities, convey a heavenly pride, and conquer all earthly fear. There are corporation executives positively miserable; there are domestic helpers who are positively victorious, because they do what they do to the glory of God—with heads held high. So it is with ministers. Their particular call is the highest call, not because people said so but because God called. Paul was emphatic about this:

> I was not called to be a missionary by any group or agency. My call is from Jesus Christ himself, and from God the Father who raised him from the dead. (Gal. 1:2 LB)

Every call or profession has its own peculiar difficulties and demands—a corporation president must show growth and profit, a doctor has long, arduous years of training—commensurate with those of the pastor. A shop owner has difficulty finding and keeping reliable employees; a lawyer may lose a case; a rancher may lose a complete harvest; a politician

13

often loses many elections before he wins one; a tradesman faces dangers of a physical nature in his work and monotony on the assembly line; a housewife feels a lack of mental stimulus and is not inspired about washing windows and waxing the kitchen floor. No call is easy if one is conscientious about doing a job well.

The call of the ministry has its problems and difficulties as well. Along with the more obvious functions, it combines the demands of nearly every profession. Scripture provides the blueprints:

> I have become all things to all men, that I might by all means save some. (1 Cor. 9:22a RSV)

> When I am with those whose consciences bother them easily, I don't act as though I know it all and don't say they are foolish; the result is that they are willing to let me help them. Yes, whatever a person is like, I try to find common ground with him so that he will let me tell him about Christ. (1 Cor. 9:22 LB)

The minister's "corporation" must show growth and balance the budget or parishioners will begin to question his leadership. His education and internship is being continually upgraded to prepare him for leadership. Other professional people take turns being on call, but a pastor's call is a twenty-four-hours-a-day, seven-day week. An owner of a business may lay off disloyal or nonproductive employees, and refuse service to those who could hinder his business.

A corporation president blames the government and stock market if his company is in the red. A physician knows that maybe some day soon a cure will be found for the disease that caused the death of a patient. A store owner can fire an employee. A rancher can await next year's harvest and a government subsidy. A tradesman can go to his union boss, who has the power to call a strike. A housewife can go shopping, move the furniture, or yell at the kids to get rid of her frustrations.

Not so with the men or women God calls into this business of shepherding. They cannot scold or admonish too much. They cannot get rid of members of their corporations who are unkind, rude, thoughtless, and destructive. They face sleepless nights wondering where they failed to help people when they know God can transform them. Once in awhile they are given a chance to see such a miracle and that's part of what the call is all about!

What constitutes a call to the ministry varies with the individual. It may be a childhood dream that continues to grow into young maturity. It may be a growing awareness or a dramatic Damascus-road call after conversion. It may even come in the middle years, after another career, when, with Luther, a person may be compelled to cry out, "I can do no other. So help me God!"

So this man called and sent by God enters that vast sub-culture of those different, a little odd, not-quite-human, and, surely, perfect creatures. His office is associated with the high priest whose lineage goes back to Aaron, Aaron's sons, and the tribe of Levi, who performed the religious functions for the people. Jesus' sacrificial life and death gave all direct access to God, but the Old Testament method carried into the early Christian Church. Although Protestants protested against priestism, they, too, fell victim to the concept, a concept that places the priest or preacher "up there," and the congregation "down here." This pedestal complex still exists, paradoxically, side by side with the concept of the humble and meek servant of God.

The lay person should be made aware that the minister is placed "up there," like a statue unveiled, when he comes to take up a new charge—then left to the elements to mar, erode, weather, and bruise. Indifferent passersby preoccupiedly ignore him or try to deface him. A pastor doesn't want to get his scars that way. He would rather be "down here" rubbing elbows with everyone else, getting the same knocks and bruises, not apart from—but a part of—life along with everyone else.

There is another serious block to understanding the call of the pastor, and it needs to be resolved. It represents the world's, not God's, portrayal of the pastor's place in society, socially and economically. This was again brought to mind recently by a famous entertainer known to all—young and old. He had been raised in a Christian environment and had reached the top in stardom. It brought some difficulties and compromises, which often occur in show business. He describes movingly in a book how he found a new relationship with Christ. As his faith deepened through the Holy Spirit, he wondered how he might best serve and discussed with his wife the possibility of the pastoral ministry:

> Honey, if I were a *preacher*, you'd still have these conflicts and problems. You'd still think I was wrong about a lot of things. You would disagree, and we would still have our personal conflicts. Our lives would be very little different—except that we wouldn't be able to give our kids the things we want to give them, and we would be living a hand-to-mouth existence. Our sphere of influence would be limited.[1]

No doubt the author made the right decision and is using his wide influence as a witness to his faith. He recognized the superimposed "job description" of the call to preach—an antiquated attitude in our enlightened space age. That is, enlightment for all segments of society except pastors. It is the poor struggling pastor in a poor struggling church concept—the idea that the world and Christian lay people have been taught for generations, that fame brings influence and reward, while obscurity and simple faithfulness have little influence and less reward.

Yet it is these thousands of insignificant, struggling pastors, living a hand-to-mouth existence through the centuries who have kept the faith and imparted it to everyone—the famous and the nobodies.

Happily, there are encouraging signs that pastors and congregations do want to know more about one another. There is a renewed interest in the ministry among young men and women, despite the complexities of the calling. Visiting the sick, baptizing, conducting funerals, and preaching, as the pastors' fundamental and only responsibilities, are of the past! Change has come to the church and to those called by God, as it has to every area of society. And that rate of change is doubling and quadrupling with startling rapidity.

The clergy, too, are swirling about, trying to find out where they are and what their immediate priorities are. Mr. John C. Harris, speaking of the ever-changing multiplicity of roles for the pastor, writes:

> What values make sense for this congregation? Who are members and what do they need? What do we expect of the pastor? . . . Beneath these questions lies a search for a new church climate—one generating fresh commitment and capable of exerting social influence in the midst of turbulent cultural change. . . . I think it is fair to say that clergy and laity are, as a rule, ineffective managers of role tensions, preferring avoidance and withdrawal to confrontation and negotiation . . . some clergy and

laity have begun to recognize that individuals by themselves are not the cause of the church's trouble. The church is caught up in a cultural crisis far beyond the power of one's pastor or one's lay board to create and sustain. . . . Rather than adversaries, clergy and laity are finding themselves allies in a common struggle.[2]

While being questioned some months ago about some of our national problems and crises, Billy Graham remarked:

I think of Jonah, who preached repentance to the people of Nineveh. The King repented and the people repented. And God spared the city of Nineveh. I think that these crises are all part of God's judgment on this country. I hear God saying we need to repent as individuals, as a Church, and as a people. . . . I think God is saying something to us. . . . We had better listen! He was trying to speak to us through the prosperous years. Now he's trying to speak to us through some judgments. And unless we do repent, unless we do turn, I think the judgment is going to get more severe and we're going to see even greater crises ahead.[3]

That's where it's at. Pastor and people have a job to do in difficult times, as Christians and believers. There is no time for spiritual self-gratification for its own sake. We are to be blessed, receive what he has to give us through his men sent by God. Together all will be the blessing he wants us to be.

But we beseech you, brethren, to respect those who labor among you and are over you in the Lord and admonish you, and to esteem them very highly in love because of their work. (1 Thess. 5:12, 13 RSV)

Checklist

_____ Honor the call—the office—of the pastor. ". . . esteem them *because of their work . . .*" (1 Thess. 5:13 RSV) Respect the man.

_____ Take him off the pedestal, and let him participate with you, as he ministers to you.

_____ Think about the roses you are sending to him. Are they wilted, thorny, faded, or dead? Begin sending roses that are beautiful, blooming, and fragrant.

_____ Do not confuse the man who is imperfect with the One who called him, who *is* perfect.

3
Questions about
HIS HUMANITY

There was a man sent from God, whose name was John. He came for testimony, to bear witness to the light, that all might believe through him. He was not the light, but came to bear witness to the light. (John 1:6, 7 RSV)

God sent a man. He did not send a superman, a supraman, nor a semidivine man. He was not 99 and 44/100 percent pure. He lived about 30 A.D. He didn't abide by custom. Instead of the usual Palestinian robe and turban, he wore animal skins sparsely and ate honey and grasshoppers. He caused a lot of criticism from religious people as well as from those in government. He raised such a stir that he lost his head. And this was the man who was divinely privileged to baptize our Lord.

Not so today, with the man God sends to pastor a group of people. He need always be above reproach, spiritual, courteous, and diplomatic. Others may make thoughtless or critical statements freely, sometimes in his presence. He becomes the sounding board of peoples' personal frustrations, probably because he represents a symbol of authority.

"I wouldn't be a minister if you paid me a million dollars!" is a comment every clergyman has heard, with or without slight variations. Those who say or think it react in several ways. One person, very much at odds with himself, his job, and his home, is on the lookout for trouble, and if he or she can't find it, makes it. He picks, pouts, criticizes, and tries to keep something stewing or tries to influence those few who pay any attention to him about everything he thinks is wrong with the church and the pastor. Of course he wouldn't be a minister for a million dollars. He couldn't stand a member like himself in his congregation!

There is another way people react to this quite common attitude (and it includes the vast majority). Generally they are sympathetic but shrug off any responsibility for making the pastor's work easier. Many don't get involved in the real where-it's-at life of the fellowship, thus ridding themselves of their obligation to minister. They attend Sunday morning worship if there is nothing more interesting to do that weekend, and this is their only participation.

Then there are those few jewels who say lovingly, "I don't see how you do it, pastor. I just couldn't do what you do, and take what you have to take." But—and this is a big one—they stand by in the wings, ready in hundreds of ways to serve the minister, his family, and their church. One positively beautiful couple comes to mind, who stop by with "roses"—gifts from trips they take, love and thank-you notes, and birthday remembrances with loads of love. They are not beneath painting the church, ushering, cooking, or helping in any way. "No" is not in their vocabulary when asked to help.

Because of the ministering of these people to their pastor, he regains a renewed sense of dignity and worth.

Again—and this will be repeated over and over—clergymen are human. What does a minister do when someone says, "You will have to come and apologize to me personally before

21

THEY CRY, TOO!

I set foot inside that church again," but that person refuses to tell the minister for what he should apologize. How does he cope with a disturbed woman who periodically comes to set him straight spiritually and then proceeds to tell this beleaguered minister all that she thinks is wrong with him and the church. Does the pastor stand by when a layman attacks his child, when the child is being normal? Or ignore a lay person who uses the telephone in a destructive way to try to convince others that this is not what "they ought to do in my church."

These are not fabricated, isolated incidents. Many were told to us in our years of traveling, as we listened to pastors and their wives. Their need to confide in someone they felt would understand was overwhelming and often full of pain.

At a conference a few months ago, a pastor related an incident that again reflected the superhuman, pedestal complex that has been conferred upon the clergy. (It is an honorary degree most ministers would prefer not to have.) Late one evening, after a particularly demanding day, he was having a cup of coffee with one of his laymen—a real pastor's layman, in a coffee shop. This man, who knew how to empathize, sensed the pastor's fatigue and discouragement. After a few minutes of kidding and frivolity, the pastor's spirits were considerably improved. As they were about to leave, a waitress came rushing toward them, waving a paper napkin. There was a message on it for the pastor. The contents on this unusual stationery disclosed a rather interesting communiqué, something to this effect: "Dear brother in Christ. I am telling you this in Christian love. . . ." And the napkin letter went on and on (it was a large napkin), soundly scolding the pastor about the length of his hair. In comparison with the long hair and beard-moustache craze his hair was quite conservative. The note continued with something about setting examples for our youth; that this kind of permissiveness by spiritual leaders was the real cause of kids' problems; that pastors ought to know better and let these obnoxious young people know that long hair was not spiritual; and so on and on. The sermon on hair closed with the words, "In Christian love."

The paradox of the whole incident was that this was a church teeming with young people, dressed in all sorts of styles, wearing all lengths of hair. Some of them, in good fun, petitioned the pastor to let his hair grow long. The only reason the pastor's hair had gotten a bit longer than he ordinarily wore it was simple. He didn't have time to get to the barber.

The layman who was with the pastor was indignant at this cowardly attack. Critical anonymity is always cowardly. But the pastor, who, through years of training had learned to keep his cool through far worse things, chuckled, "I must not be doing much of a job lately. I haven't been taken to task 'in Christian love' for quite awhile. Beware when all men speak well of you." The layman did not take it so lightly. He couldn't understand what he considered judgmental rudeness, when he knew his pastor was so busy taking care of the needs of others that he didn't have time for a haircut.

When a congregation chooses a man to serve as its pastor, expectation naturally is high on both sides. The church expects him to be a wise leader, who will be a perfect minister for their needs. The pastor also has his ideals. He feels sure that in this new situation he will profit from past ministries and looks forward to achieving new goals. There is the usual honeymoon, during which time everyone puts his best foot forward. It doesn't take long to discover that in this new marriage there are imperfections in each partner. The minister is not perfect and is not an expert in everything expected of him. The minister discovers the weaknesses of the congregation and sees their need for maturity. Perhaps he is more realistic than lay people, because he knows there are no perfect people, including himself, and no perfect churches!

This is a man sent by God. Sometimes he doesn't have time

to call on all the sick and the shut-ins, spend the time he ought to for his own personal and spiritual needs, and prepare for the unending demands of preaching and teaching. He cannot split himself into enough segments to attend all meetings, dinners, social gatherings, youth functions; to administrate the budget, fix broken faucets in rest rooms, try to eat with his family one night a week, and find time for a haircut.

By and large, church members still expect the clergy to perform their religious duties for them. After a pastor has gone to theological school, been ordained and licensed to preach, it is assumed that he knows all there is to know about the ever-growing ministerial haberdashery. That he will be able to wear expertly the increasing number of hats thrust upon his head in the ever-widening areas of pastoral responsibilities.

Throughout Scripture there were many men sent and chosen by God for a particular ministry. Abraham, Noah, Jacob, Saul, David, Solomon, Isaiah, Joseph, Peter, John, Paul—all were men, human beings. All had imperfections. Many sinned greatly in God's sight, but he used them anyway. A priest, a rabbi, a pastor, a minister, a shepherd, a preacher, whatever they are called—all are fallible. It is the message to which they bear witness that is infallible. Yet many believers, communicants, Christians, church members get the two all mixed up. It was to the masses on the hillside that Jesus spoke: "But you are to be perfect, even as your Father in heaven is perfect." (Matt. 5:48 LB) This is not for preachers only. No one is exempt.

Jesus' imperative nullifies the conscious or unconscious rationalizing, lay people should be working at being a little bit perfect, but the minister should be a whole lot perfect. Outwardly, there is not a believer, or church member, who, if asked, "Do you expect your pastor to be perfect? Is it possible that he is capable of making mistakes?" would not agree that, of course he is not perfect and does make mistakes. But heaven help him when he does!

Paul, in his first letter to young pastor Timothy, lays down some high principles for pastors. (1 Tim. 3:1–7) Don't stop your reading there. He goes right down the line with deacons, elders, and church members. The straight talk in his letters was directed primarily to lay members. Paul showed much concern for his young pastors and sent instructions to the church about their care.

The Reverend Mr. Stuart P. Benson, a minister to ministers, in an article entitled "The Making and Breaking of Pastors and Churches," writes:

> Every pastor makes mistakes. He, like the members of his church, is only human. Church members are inclined to pass lightly over their own faults but to hold the pastor rigidly accountable for his. He is expected to be above reproach in word and deed, but it does not take long to discover that he, too, is a child of Adam. A church that is willing to try to save the pastor when he has made a mistake will not only save a man for the ministry but experience a rich return for being gracious.[1]

One of the most difficult aspects of the ministry should be discussed at this point. It is a built-in hazard. It strains the minister's humanity, and makes him vulnerable to criticism or hostility because of seeming oversight and preoccupation. Some call this "gear-shifting." It involves many different kinds of ministering and the meeting of all kinds of needs within a short time span. It involves running the gamut of emotions, and entering into and becoming a part of each mood and situation—and it happens to everyone.

THEY CRY, TOO!

A housewife may decide to sew a dress. She lays out a pattern on some fabric, begins to cut, and the phone rings. The school calls to say Jimmy is ill, would she please come and get him. She dashes to his school, gets him home, attends to his needs, and the doorbell rings. She impatiently gets rid of a salesman so she can concentrate on more important things. Suddenly she remembers that she has asked friends in for the evening and for a late dessert. She rushes to the store for groceries. There is dinner to cook, the dog to feed, phone calls to make for the PTA, and the house to straighten up for her guests. If someone had tried to visit with her at the market, she might have ducked into another aisle, since she was in a hurry. If her best, but most talkative, friend should call, she would have to excuse herself, perhaps somewhat curtly. She may not have seen someone she knew, who waved at her on the way to the market. Her carefully planned day has boomeranged completely. She didn't fulfill responsibilities to a sick friend she had promised to see. In her rushing around, without intending to be, since she was preoccupied, she may have appeared to be rude and insensitive.

A man leaves for his office early in the morning. His car has a flat tire, and he calls the garage. He had anticipated getting some work done before the office opened, but he is forty-five minutes late. There are ten phone messages on his desk. He sorts out one or two that seem the most important just then. Repairmen come into his office to fix something and make nerve-racking noises while he tries to finish a report for the noon deadline. His wife decides that this is the day she will stop by and have lunch with him. He explains that this is impossible and she leaves angrily. He goes down the hall to the accounting office and impatiently refuses a cup of coffee with Joe. Our harassed businessman glowers at the next person he meets, not really seeing him. The report is not finished, and he is called into his boss's office. After a long conference, his secretary reminds him that his wife's birthday is the next day. He dashes to the department store just before it closes and in his upset state can't understand why they don't have more courteous salesgirls. He is late for dinner, yells at the kids for being too noisy, and his wife is still unhappy with him.

A comedy of errors, which is not the fault of either of these two individuals. They had to "gear-switch" all day long, and, in the process, seemed discourteous, preoccupied, and unaware of others with whom they had contact.

Fortunately, between understanding friends, good relationships are soon restored when the pressure is off. Everyone has days like that. Generally we forgive and overlook what seems to be negligence and rudeness when we know the circumstances.

Then why so much elaboration about "gear-shifting"? The very important point to be made here is that if a pastor is guilty of things like preoccupation, rudeness, tardiness, forgetting something, or not returning a phone call, Christian people, who should be most understanding, are not. One of the questions, given to a sampling of a hundred lay people in three churches with three different denominations, was: "If, in your estimation, the pastor makes a mistake, or is seemingly negligent to you or someone close to you, how would you feel?" The answers were honest. Some were vague, some indicated they'd not bother the pastor, but they would feel cool towards him. Too high a percentage admitted they would be hurt.

This was brought home again, some months ago, when I addressed a group of women in a church in another city. After the meeting I met a young woman whom I had known some years before, who was now a member of that church. As we visited, she expressed herself freely—that she liked the church and community, but the minister was unfriendly. I knew him well, he was an especially warm person, so this came as quite a shock. She explained that a few days before she had stopped by the church to get something. At the same time the pastor came out of his office, smiled, and asked "How are you?"

"I answered 'fine,' " she continued, "but he was so preoccupied that he didn't really see me!" Any sort of explanation I volunteered was rejected by her, because she was bent on hugging her hurt.

Naturally I was concerned about this episode, and that evening I asked the pastor if he was aware of how she felt. He was surprised by her reaction. He explained that on that particular day, before 6:00 A.M., he had received a phone call from the emergency ward of a hospital. There had been an accident, and a young woman had been killed. The young man who was driving was a member of his church, and in critical condition. The pastor went to the hospital immediately. When he returned to his office, his secretary was nervously waiting, wondering if he would get to the mortuary on time for a memorial service. Back to the office again, without breakfast or lunch, and there on the desk a message to return a call marked "urgent"! The chairman of the finance committee wanted to know which bills to pay or to leave unpaid this month. A young couple waited and watched the clock. It was their lunch hour, and they were there for premarital counseling. Another call, from the wife of a sick man. He was not in a critical condition, but she was irate over the fact that the pastor had not yet called on her husband.

Books and notes were scattered all around, and as he looked at the disarray, he wondered in fatigue and discouragement when he would be able to get back to his sermon preparation. Another call came from the hospital. The young man was responding, though still on the critical list, and wanted to see his pastor. He did not know if this would be his last chance to talk with the young man. He dashed out of his office to get to the hospital. It was at that moment the young woman walked down the hall of the church. The fact that he was collected enough to smile and say anything to her at all was a miracle. Of course he was preoccupied. Now, in addition to his guilt feeling about not getting everything done, he had another problem. What could he do to help win her confidence again?

Dozens of times each day a minister is torn apart, shifting gears from one emotion to another: joy over the birth of a baby; despair over a marriage torn apart. Always he is concerned about someone's need. That tragedy, this grief, worry over financial concerns in the church or in his home, and his family's need for him. Last, but not least, there is no time for his own needs. Not every day for a pastor is like the one just described, but many of them are.

A minister wrote an editorial for a religious publication, entitled "What's Wrong with Ministers?" Here is part of it:

> A perennial question was tossed to me on one of my recent preaching missions. "Why are ministers so wacky?" You'll notice this is in the same category as "When did you stop beating your wife?" But, for the sake of argument, let us allow the assumption.
>
> One of the reasons that ministers tend to be wacky is that the demands are immense. I use the word immense in the technical sense of "immensus," that is, that which can be understood to a degree, but not completely, with our finite categories of thought. No one, least of all the minister, can know what it is he's supposed to be or what he's supposed to do, because he takes his color and his self-understanding, at least in a real sense, from the people he's called to serve. He is essentially a lover and an enabler of love. Now love can be a touchy subject, and most people are totally bewildered and confused both about their feelings and about how they can be safely manifested. Enter confusion.
>
> The physician, the psychiatrist, the various quasi-

shrinks, the lawyer, the dentist, the businessman and
the manufacturer all have clear-cut job descrip-
tions. . . . Seldom are they forced to make a
professional response on the basis of personal
emotion and love.

But the gospel is overtly about emotions. It's
about joy, ecstasy, fear, dread, guilt, loneliness, and
personal involvement in all of these. Naturally,
ministers are going to be a little wacky with this kind
of a crucible in which they must constantly perform.

When you consider what it means to be in touch
with the Holy Spirit in terms of what love means in
the context of the gospel, it is the most exciting and
profoundly precious thing that could happen. . . .
But because the ministry is so intimate and
profound, it is relatively rare that a person should be
able to turn on everybody. We must lower our
expectations, rather than glibly assuming that all
ministers are nuts and should not be taken seriously.
You'd be nuts too if you were facing the same 24-
hour life and death pressures every day from
hundreds of people, each one of whom had different
rights and different expectations.

Be kind. Take a preacher to lunch this week.[2]

A missionary, home on furlough, was invited to speak to a
group of ministers and their wives. She had personality plus,
was highly intelligent, and a commanding speaker. Her
audience settled back, expecting to hear experiences from her
field of foreign service. Having been at the conference from its
beginning, she must have sensed among these spiritual leaders
some of their feelings of inadequacy, loneliness, and failure in
not being able to do everything that was required of them.

When she got up to speak, instead of referring to her work,
she addressed herself to them. She gave a message of praise

and gratefulness for their love and support. Then, in a moment full of deep empathy, she said:

> So many of our Christian church members need a "monk" to do their repentance for them. You are more spiritual if you drive an old car, don't wear expensive clothes, live in a small house, don't show emotion when you want to belt somebody, and you may have every right to, but if you do lose your temper or say anything that borders on talking about someone, it's much worse than if one of your congregation does it. Both because they believe it's a no-no for you and because you feel you shouldn't.

She closed by reminding them about the greatest opportunity in history for world evangelism—the largest mission field—our own country. She then led in fervent prayer that these pastors would be blessed with growing Christians, that they wouldn't have to spend their valuable and overworked time in dealing with pettiness but in the larger work of true pastoring—enabling others to minister.

Her final plea was eloquent: "Lord, instead of having to be an example, let each of these dear servants be an opportunity."

Checklist

_____ Realize with your feelings and mind that your pastor is decidedly human. Then accept that humanness.

_____ Be conciliatory and understanding about a mistake or oversight. Let him know kindly rather than telling others about it. You will feel better. He won't be adding to his mountain-of-things-I-didn't-get-done guilt, and you will have new love and respect for each other.

31

_____ When you feel sent to discuss something with your pastor, be sure you are sent by the right Spirit. Distinguish between venting hostility and seeking constructive help.

_____ If there is something about him you don't like, go to him, and between the two of you, you may be able to discover why. Ask yourself if you have to accept everything about yourself, spouse, kids, and friends to like them. If you make allowances for them, should you do less for him?

_____ If your pastor passes you by without noticing you or is preoccupied, why don't you ask God's blessing and help as he attends to another task or crisis. Remember the key word—"gear-shifting"!

_____ Save yourself time. Don't write anonymous letters. Your minister usually looks for the name of the writer before reading the letter. When you have occasion to write, the proper salutation is not "Dear Reverend." "Dear Mr.," or "Mrs.," or "Dr.," and the last name, are proper.

_____ Invite your pastor out for coffee on the spur of the moment and get to know one another better.

_____ If your pastor should drop in on you or see you in public, where you may be engaging in a "vice" you think he may disapprove of, don't hide it. He may not disapprove. He would like to be treated like any of your friends and to feel free to drop in on you at any time.

_____ If there are young people in your household, teach them, by good example, how to relate to their minister. Your attitude will become their attitude.

4
Questions about
HIS *NEEDS*

Throughout this book, the various subjects dealt with use the same title, with the exception of the last word. That word indicates the emphasis of the chapter. In this chapter, however, the second to the last word needs just as much, if not more, emphasis. Why you should ask about *his* needs. The long-held view of a minister, rabbi, priest, or pastor is that he has an infallible, unending pipeline of wisdom, knowledge, and power that comes naturally to him and not to ordinary folks. He just opens a faucet and pours out divine blessings for all the needs of those for whom he is responsible.

There is some evidence that this view may be changing. Pastor and people are beginning to see the need for interaction on the same level—to see that they should grow and tackle personal, church, and societal problems together as partners. Still, in the minds of many, this man sent by God, up there in the pulpit, is sort of unlike those in the pews. He really is a bit strange and different. There is an unawareness that he is a person, and has the same feelings and needs as everyone else.

A startling clue, revealing just how unaware of this people are, was again brought to light in a pastors' wives get-together. The opportunity for these women to share with each other is rare, so when it does occur it is significant.

This is, in essence, a distillation of the confessions and feelings of most of these ladies:

> I didn't realize that I, too, had the typical image that most people have about my minister-husband. You see, I expected him to be just that: minister and husband, in that order, twenty-four hours a day, year in and year out, forever. He should direct all of our family's devotional life (letting me off the hook), always leave home happy and whistling, even if I was ugly to him before he left. He'd better not be late for dinner again, always be courteous and kind, never lose his cool (I could, you understand) with the children and with me. And on one of his rare evenings at home, he must do what I want to do. If he expresses weariness, discouragement, frustration or anger, he isn't being "spiritual." That was O.K. for the rest of us. You see, he really isn't a man—a husband or a father—like other men. He's "on duty" twenty-four hours a day.

This "confession," with slight variations, led to a good deal of self-searching and penitence for what we knew was selfishness in many of us. We renewed our dedication to make our homes a place where our husbands, not minister-husbands, could be themselves, where they would be treated as *men*.

One of the women wrote sometime later:

> I can't believe how little our family understood the impossibility of carrying out all pastoral duties during our many years in churches. It's been a

difficult effort but now we have a better understanding. My husband is learning to say no to less important things and spend more time at home. He didn't need the pressures we were putting on him, in addition to those hundreds who don't understand his needs at all!

If this situation can prevail in a minister's home, how much more magnified are the attitudes of the people and the community he serves. Serving others' needs is a large part of his vocation. A church congregation has a limited right to expect many and varied kinds of serving from their pastor. He is more than willing to attempt to be all things to all people. But a satisfying marriage is a two-way street. Both partners realize that they each have needs. In a sense, pastor and people are married.

What are some of your pastor's needs? They are the needs of every person born. God sent a man to minister to you. This man has the physical needs of all men. He gets tired, hungry. He has creative needs, sexual needs. He feels all emotions known to all men. He feels pain, discouragement, inadequacy, fear, doubt, jealousy, neglect, anger, and, at times, feels unloved, lonely, and unappreciated. *He cries, too!*

He listens by the hour to those who come to him for his help and understanding of their burdens and problems. Surely he will have the answers. He has it all put together. It is difficult for these troubled ones to comprehend that he also needs someone to lean on at times. If he expresses normal emotions, it may be shocking. If he shares doubt, some are shaken. If he hints that in trying times he feels unloved or unappreciated, it must be self-pity or an ego problem. This may not be an intentional reaction. This insensitivity and unawareness results from long-established thought form and tradition.

One of your minister's basic needs is for *understanding*—by his wife, his family, his staff, his friends, his congregation. He is automatically expected to understand his people's actions and problems, and the unlovable behavior of a few who like to keep turmoil going in the church.

Thank goodness for the gift of understanding manifested by some beautiful sheep in the flock. Paul must have had some wonderfully understanding friends in the church at Phillipi. It is a love letter that he writes them, without the toughness manifested in some of his other letters:

> All my prayers for you are full of praise to God! When I pray for you my heart is full of joy, because of all your wonderful help in making known the Good News. . . . How natural it is that I should feel as I do about you, for you have a very special place in my heart. . . . Only God knows how deep is my love and longing for you. . . . May you always be doing these good, kind things which show that you are a child of God. (Phil. 1:3–11 LB)

His feelings are eloquently stated in the King James translation: "I thank my God upon every remembrance of you." (Phil. 1:3 AV) Every time Paul thought of certain Christians, members of the Phillipian congregation, a warm glow enveloped him. He forgot about the cold, damp, dark cell in which he was imprisoned.

He remembered only those wonderful people who laid it on the line for him in spite of the Roman hostility toward this new radical religion, which could not be squelched!

There are modern Phillipians whose every remembrance brings that same feeling Paul experienced. Immediately there comes to mind a man, who surely was "sent by God," named Frank Allen. Frank is ninety-eight years young! He has been in his present church for uncountable years. He is a beautiful person. No one remembers that he was ever different. Faithful (nothing can keep him away from his beloved church), loyal, positive, uncomplaining and totally undemanding. He is the kind of member a pastor would like to have ask a favor because of the joy and spirit that he imparts. He has had more than his share of grief, illness, tragedy, but no one would ever know. His smile and his handclasp are warm and strong. He loves his church and his pastor in a special way.

Some years ago, when a young pastor was new to his church, Frank Allen asked him to call. Coming from him, the request was unusual. The pastor knew that Frank had been privileged to grow into Christian maturity under some great ministers. Therefore he was, not surprisingly, apprehensive. He was well aware that to wear their shoes was going to be difficult. But he had come to love Frank Allen's great spirit and respect his advice. He wondered where he might have slipped up, or if he had upset someone, or omitted something important. Almost hoping there would be no one home, the pastor knocked on the door. He was greeted cordially and invited in. This elderly church statesman made him feel at ease immediately and began to ask a lot of questions about his personal needs and about his family. This, too, was unusual, for a pastor is supposed to initiate conversations. The pastor waited for the shoe to drop. It never did. Wonder of wonders, this dear man *ministered* to his pastor. He told about his personal faith, how God had blessed him through triumph and defeat. He told how every day of his life he prayed for his church and his pastor, as he sensed the awesomeness of his new pastor's responsibility. He wanted to know how he could help lessen the burdens.

Then this usually soft-spoken, gentle man raised his voice with a loving firmness, "Young man, you are working much too hard. You didn't need to tell me that you don't take a day off. I knew it! You must take time off, regularly. Your family needs you, and you need time for yourself. God does not expect you to kill yourself for the sake of the Gospel. You are much more useful to him *alive!* And I am going to do whatever I can." Together they had prayer. Frank Allen prayed for his pastor.

The pastor knew that this man meant what he said. He left with a spring in his step that gave him courage for some difficult months of change ahead. Frank Allen is still serving. Although he is more frail, the pastor knows that he is supportive and praying. Not an "Oh, that's right, I must remember to pray for the pastor" kind of prayer. He has a deep, close relationship with his Lord and there is no doubt that they are on intimate speaking terms. When he prays, one knows it and feels it. Not too long ago, when the church asked for helpers in vacation Bible school, hundreds of others paid no heed. But Frank volunteered, and how the little ones loved him! It must have seemed just about like having Jesus there, holding them on his lap.

When a new plan of action or a new program is proposed to the church, people half Frank's age, afraid of anything new, drag their feet and voice their negative feelings. Not so with Frank! He always voices positives and says, much louder than he ordinarily speaks, "I think we ought to try it. We need to be looking ahead ten, twenty, or thirty years. We'd better change with the rest of the world." At ninety-eight, looking ahead thirty years! Just before this book was sent to the publisher, this letter came from Frank.

> Dear Pastor,
> I am sorry I forgot your birthday. Pastor, I am sure glad you are going to be with us longer—praise God for that. God has wonderfully blessed our church through your preaching and management. I thank God for you and for all of your family. . . .

I never was in a church where the fellowship was so warm and filled with love for one another. How I enjoy the messages and fellowship of all the congregation. I can feel the Spirit of God in the people, My soul is warmed and lifted up at every meeting.

I have a bad cold, so I have missed three Sundays. How my soul longed for the love and fellowship of the church. . . . Express my love to all the people. Now may the love of God the Father, Son, and Holy Spirit abide with us all, now and forever.

> Your brother in Christ,
> Frank Allen

Loving understanding! Frank's new job is working with youth.

Earlier there was a reference to Paul's exceptional qualifications for pastors in 1 Timothy. These, a minister cannot hope to attain by himself. He must be absolutely dependent upon Christ and the continuing work of the Holy Spirit to keep him in tune as he tries to live up to Paul's ten commandments for pastors. He is, in a sense, at the mercy of those to whom he ministers. They hold the key to making or breaking a pastor's spirit and his ability to minister. Those to whom he ministers can unlock reservoirs of dynamic, powerful energy through *prayer*, the pastor's greatest need—for himself, for his family, and for the church. *This everyone can do if they cannot do anything else!* If people are not praying he knows it. If people are praying, he *feels* it.

Prayer is a power. It produces energy. A new phenomenon for Americans is the energy crisis caused by devouring overconsumption and dwindling supply. But pastors have had a perpetual energy crisis. If people could realize how much energy is dissipated by their pastor as he attends to destructive, devastating, and debilitating pettinesses in his parish. To add to his energy crisis is the factor of underproduction in a readily available source—intercessory prayer.

Why is every writing of Paul generously interlaced with pleas, petitions, and emotional appeals for prayer?

> Pray much for others; plead for God's mercy upon them. Pray in this way for kings and all others who are in authority over us or are in places of high responsibility. . . . (1 Tim. 2:1, 2 LB)

If we had taken Paul seriously and prayed unceasingly, meaningfully, for those in places of high responsibility, is it possible that we might have prayed a protective shield around these men and neutralized the power of the evil one, to whom some of them succumbed? How often do you, do I, pray for those in high places? Our president, our leaders, our pastors?

Let's be honest. Isn't it much easier to complain and criticize and take potshots at them? You bet it is. It also affords us a chance to become righteously indignant devotees of the I-told-you-so cult, which enjoys seeing the high brought down low. Our sinful nature causes us to take delight when the famous, the rich, the talented, the symbols of authority are brought down to our level. Lower than our level would be more delightful! If you do not believe in a satanic force at work, there is food for thought.

But *prayer!* That takes something else. That takes discipline, a forgiving spirit, a concern for others, self-searching, a pretty good friendship with the One to whom we pray, and a good talking and listening relationship, so that we can come to him boldly! That means we have to know each other like old-time friends. "Oh yes, God, I guess I ought to be praying," is not going to cut the mustard. God won't take us seriously, any more than the neighbor with whom we have a "hi," once-a-week relationship.

Church members slip into a dangerous syndrome periodically. They begin to rationalize their lack of spiritual vitality and try to put it on their leaders. "If only we had a really inspired preacher." "If church weren't so dull." "If 'they' would be personally concerned about me." "If they'd do thus and so in that church maybe I'd be inspired to pray." They've got it all backwards. They want all the blessings first—then maybe they'll pray. It doesn't work that way. This attitude produces not *energy* but *crisis!* Instead of running on nervous energy, we can plug into God's energy. There's no limit to his supply. Besides which, God doesn't place embargoes or raise the price. You pay the price when your spiritual needs exceed your spiritual supply. It's up to you to keep the pipeline open, and you will get more spiritual energy than you need for any crisis—with lots left over for others.

The Apostle James probably didn't get a Ph.D. in psychology, but he had profound insights about the therapeutic results of praying for others. "Admit your faults to one another and pray for each other so that *you* may be healed." (Jas. 5:16 LB) Spiritually, physically, emotionally. "The earnest prayer of a righteous man has great power and wonderful results." (Jas. 5:16 LB) One would be foolish not to heed such good advice. Try it. You'll like it! You'll survive any energy crisis.

We have been dealing with a minister's need for prayer—his crude oil for refined energy! It would be a colossal oversight to leave out a discussion of his physical energy. The clergy do not take care of their health as they should. Most confide that they do not have regular checkups—not because of fear for their own health but, tragically, for fear of their future ministry and the security of their families if they should discover a health problem. Pastors do not have the health protection that other professional and working people do. There is the ever-present specter of being branded ineffective as a pastor or of having to leave his life's work.

The church he is serving gets uneasy, and churches who might have wanted him as their pastor decide his fate for him. He is considered a poor risk. He won't be able to work the excessively long days churches have come to expect. It is a serious and fearful problem that haunts every minister I know.

The person who works an eight-hour, five-day week can go on with his job indefinitely. His coworkers are pleased; he has time to recuperate and go back to work refreshed. But a pastor's ten-to-fourteen-hour, seven-day week hinders complete recuperation and jeopardizes his career.

In all fairness, many churches have been generous and gracious for months and sometimes years to pastors with serious illnesses. Though fully recuperated, the remembrance of a pastor's health setback makes a congregation uneasy.

There are times when a pastor needs to know that somebody else besides God *loves* him. That love needs some people on it! Love is the essence of his life, his ministry, his very reason for being—a man sent by God. He is to preach that God is Love. That God so loved the world. . . . Love is what he must impart to the troubled, the sick, the grieving, the broken, the discouraged in a multitude of ways. He must take an intangible word and put meaning and reality into it.

There are thousands of clergymen who have little active love shown them. It's not because people don't want to. They don't know how to love a minister. They are not aware that this man sent by God—the enabler of God's love—needs it as much as they do. Clergymen themselves sometimes don't realize that they, too, have a right to receive love. But they do know when it is missing. They wonder what it is about their ministry, themselves, their church, their purpose, that seems to fall so short of the expectations they had when they entered their profession.

Not long ago a friend who was going through our city stopped by for a visit. He was a big outdoor man, a strong Christian, and a leading layman in his church. He was enthusiastic about the coming of a new pastor several years before.

"He's done a fantastic job," this friend observed. "We all think the world of him. But lately he doesn't seem to have the same punch he had at first; he seems discouraged. We are puzzled about it. We all really love him."

"Have you ever told him that?" asked my husband.

Red from embarrassment this big hunk of a man mumbled, "Of course not."

"Why don't you try it sometime?"

The man became silent and no more was said about it.

Some time later we read about some interesting happenings in the news bulletin from his church. In the ensuing weeks we sensed a new spirit in that fellowship, and it sprang to life from a printed page. The pastor's messages to his congregation were full of · new excitement and expectation for the future. Attendance had increased and love seemed to flow out of the paper. A news item appeared weekly, and church members expressed the love of Christ and his Spirit, as they experienced it, in a new way. There was no mistaking the fruit of the Spirit—*love.*

Nearly a year after his first visit, our friend knocked on our door once again.

He said, "I just had to stop and tell you what's happening."

"I think we know," I answered, "it shows."

We sat down. He talked without stopping for two hours. He referred to his previous visit and the suggestion that was made about expressing love to his pastor.

"I finally got the courage to do it. Can you imagine me telling another man, 'I love you'? I always thought that was his job. Well, I mumbled through it, and I must admit he looked at me a bit curiously. I looked down at the floor and when I looked up at him again there were tears in his eyes. 'I think that was the first time in my eighteen years in the pastorate that anyone besides my family had told me that.'

"Man, that started the ball rolling. The next Sunday I told him again. Others heard it and mumbled it real shy at first. Then we began to tell it to each other. Men telling men, and women telling everybody! Pretty soon someone got this idea for a 'love feast,' to let our pastor know that we meant it. We loved him all the time, but we didn't let him know. The next thing you know everybody in the church got the 'disease.' Things just haven't been the same, and we hope they never will be again. We're even loving a few people who gripe and complain about everything. They're unhappy, but we're going to love them into happiness."

A revolution? Yes! A love revolution! Because one great big awkward self-conscious man was courageous enough to say, "Hey, pastor, I love you."

Another need your minister has is the need for *appreciation* and, closely related, *praise.* Countless times, week in and week out, a pastor wonders if he is getting through. Or if he is fulfilling his purpose in God's ministry; if there is any evidence of Christians growing into maturity.

The minister is expected to give out loads of appreciation. He is to use honey, not vinegar, in his preaching; discretion in meetings; loving understanding with difficult and unlovable people. He must praise and thank those who serve on committees; decorate the church; and compliment the choir and soloist if they sing flat. If he thanks a list of people for some task done, and inadvertently misses someone, woe be unto him. The phone will soon be ringing in his home or in his office, but probably not before it has rung in the homes of others to relay the terrible oversight. We tend to forget that the purpose of service is a part of our discipleship responsibility. Tasks that are viewed as a pastor's *job*, but lay people's *option.*

Words of appreciation or praise are often late in coming, if at all, from the majority of lay people. At a convention, a pastor confided that some of his closest friends, after six years in the parish, had not once thanked or praised him for a sermon or a blessing received.

"Now I know that in six years there just had to be one commendable sermon," he laughed, half-heartedly. These were some of the dearest, kindest people he knew, but it did not occur to them to praise or thank him for his ministry to them and their children.

Many expect the pastor to know, by osmosis, that they are appreciative, and they are. Some people praise him readily to others, but he needs to know it, too. Perhaps some can't express gratitude, because they do not have a thankful spirit. We cannot give away what we do not have.

Everyone needs to feel appreciated. It is a psychologically sound principle that when anyone receives praise—a child, an adolescent, an employee, a marriage partner, a student, a minister—all work harder, with new resolve to do better.

Here are some comments from three clergymen who expressed feeling a lack of appreciation from their congregations:

> The laity has grown complacent. They have become a hindrance to the true aims of the church.

> I feel unworthy to guide people. I could make a better contribution outside the church.

> My role seems to be an exercise in futility. I hate the loneliness.[1]

They are saying, in different ways, "If I could feel appreciated, loved, and feel the confidence of my people, it would again seem worthwhile."

Our ultimate ideal, whether in the pew or the pulpit, is to be committed enough to Christ so that whatever we do is what God expects of us. It is not for the praise of men, but when the task is done for our Lord, it is not wrong to receive encouragement from people. Look at the salutation in every one of Paul's letters. He knew how to get the attention of the believers, though he often scolded them soundly. He began with some sugar and honey praise and gratitude.

Jesus experienced ingratitude when, after healing ten men, only one returned to thank him. He was hurt enough to ask where the others were. He cried openly and unashamedly over his beloved Jerusalem. "I wanted to hold you and love you. I tried to give you new Life, and you could have cared less."

Could you imagine how vital a love relationship would be with your spouse, your fiancé, your children, your parents, if your only words to them were corrective? If there were no praise for a job well done and no expression of appreciation? Are they supposed to assume that you care? God sent a man who has need for *praise* and *appreciation.* He needs to know people care.

Confidence in the pastor's leadership is another vital need. He is asked to serve a congregation in the capacity of spiritual leader. He is called upon to bring into play his education, experience, talents, sensitivity, and professional ability. Yet, having come into a church with these qualifications, there are a few who would deny him the respect and right to implement them. They believe that they know his business better than he does.

As with other leaders, pastors are entitled to rewards as well as recriminations, praise as well as criticism, joy as well as judgment. Speaking about this kind of vulnerability, one of our late outspoken presidents commented tartly, "If you don't like the heat, stay out of the kitchen."[2] He didn't seem to mind the heat, because he stayed in it quite a while. Most clergymen don't want to leave their "kitchens" either.

They like their work!

They like the sense of purpose and the creative demands that stimulate the mind and spirit. However, there are marked differences between secular and religious professions. Secular leaders are able to relieve some of the pressures and the kitchen heat. They can make many of their own decisions, fire people who are not doing the job, and hire others. This is not so for the pastor. He must make decisions with the consent of a large group of people. He cannot fire troublemakers or the unproductive, whether staff or lay members. It would seem that Christ's people would want to help keep the kitchen cool, but some like it hot! Some don't even bother to call the fire department.

A pastor's wife shared an experience that caused her much distress. It was disturbing to discover this usually cheerful woman's hurt:

"I've had it. I couldn't tell Dick about what happened at the last women's business meeting I attended. The women were discussing plans for the coming year. One woman suggested the need for Bible study in our church. The church has hundreds of people every week in Bible classes. I've seen her visiting in the corridor during the study hour. That didn't get to me as much as her thoughtless remark, 'The trouble with the church is . . .' I know who she meant by 'the church.' "

"The trouble with the church is . . . !" The most devastating statement for those caught up in churchianity. Those who say this attack themselves. They *are* the church! They should say, *"The trouble with me is . . ."* Usually they make a presumption without information. The person making the statement hasn't bothered to check out what has been done, is being done, or is being planned, on the very issue he or she has in mind.

How different from other Christians, who live their faith. Like the Phillippian Christians they look for the good:

> We feel so privileged to have such a wonderful church. Our children are so happy here. And we are growing. What can we do to make it better?[3]

Music to everyone—especially their pastor.

Another need of a pastor is the need for *loyalty*. Not only from his members but from his staff, his committees, boards, elders, and deacons. Differing on a proposal is different from being disloyal, disagreeable, and divisive. If staff and board members cannot give unequivocal loyalty to their pastor and church, they should have the integrity to resign from office. The damage one disloyal person can cause cannot be measured. Unfortunately, it happens—too often!

> There you are, quarreling about whether I am greater than Appollos, and dividing the church. Doesn't this show how little you have grown in the Lord? (1 Cor. 3:4 LB)
>
> If anyone is causing divisions among you, he should be given a first and second warning. After that have nothing more to do with him. (Titus 3:10 LB)
>
> Don't listen to complaints against the pastor unless there are two or three witnesses to accuse him. (1 Tim. 5:19 LB)
>
> We beg you, brothers, to acknowledge those who are working so hard among you, and in the Lord's fellowship are your leaders and counsellors. Hold them in the highest possible esteem and affection for the work they do. (1 Thess. 5:12 NEB)

This is a book about basic courtesy to ministers. Nothing said thus far is as respectful and kind as giving your minister your loyalty. It is good etiquette. It is profoundly Christian. It takes so little and produces so much. If you cannot give loyalty, go to a church where you can practice this virtue.

Your pastor is many things. Sometimes weak and strong, quiet and gregarious, spiritual and unspiritual, certain and uncertain, dedicated and wavering, saintly and earthy, loftily inspired and defeatedly discouraged, carried to the heights, plummeted to the depths. Do you hold him in the "highest possible esteem and affection" or do you plunge, him into the valley of your discontent? This man sent by God.

Checklist

_____ Before you can help meet some of your pastor's needs, think about your needs. His are the same.

_____ If your church is calling a new pastor, do everything you can those first days and weeks to make him feel welcome. A clean home on his arrival, a grocery shower, a plant, coffee and doughnuts—these will help him during a difficult time of loneliness and apprehension.

_____ Though his work requires your minister to be aggressive and outgoing, he may not be that way naturally. Take him off the hook. You be the aggressor and express concern and love for him.

_____ Many ask if they should invite him and his wife (maybe the children) to dinner, since he has few free evenings. Yes! By all means! His wife will enjoy not cooking, and you may all discover a treasure chest of friendship.

_____ Avoid the phrase, "The trouble with the church is . . ."

_____ Show concern for his health. Insist your minister have hours somewhat like those in the congregation. If but a few items in these checklists were to be implemented, he would enjoy glorious health!

_____ Respect your minister's dinner hour with his family. Allow him to eat without telephone interruptions between the hours of 5:30 and 7 P.M. You will contribute immeasurably to his physical and emotional health. You will give his family a chance to have Dad all to themselves for that little while.

_____ Suggest the church give your pastor periodic times away—for a conference he would like to attend, or to rest and study away by himself. Some churches take a leaf out of the educators' book, and allow sabbatical leaves after a given period of time in the service of the church.

_____ Show your *understanding, love, appreciation, praise, confidence, prayer* and *loyalty* in a tangible way.

5
Questions about
HIS FRIENDSHIP

During the past year a major religious body held a series of conferences in different areas of our country, to which clergymen, denominational leaders, and executives were invited. The pastors were asked to discuss their frustrations, fears, feelings, and financial problems.

The theme that kept coming up was that of *loneliness*. A song popular several years ago begins: "People who need people are the luckiest people in the world." It might be paraphrased to describe the feelings of these men: "Pastors do need people. They're the loneliest people in the world."

Some of the pastor's needs have been discussed, but there is one that should be looked at separately—the overriding need of clergymen for *friends*. These men are expected to be a friend to everyone—but *few are friends to them*. It is easy to love the lovable. Your pastor, more than anyone, is asked to be a friend to and love the unlovable. Jesus spoke strongly of this:

And whenever a village [a church member?] won't accept you or listen to you, shake off the dust from your feet as you leave; it is a sign that you have abandoned it to its fate. (Mark 6:11 LB)

This is plain talk from our Lord.

"You have done what you could," he is saying. "Don't waste your energies with those who will have none of it. Utilize your time and energies to better advantage on those who really want to hear about God's love for them. God loves the others, too, but they've had their chance."

Today's pastor faces a dilemma. Should *he* give up on them? Ministers spend needless time and energy on Christian believers who are unlovable and do not want to change. Where does the pastor go when he needs a friend to help him get his priorities and perspectives back?

God needed friends. Look at the friendships in his Book. Is there any more poignant than that of David and Jonathan? Esther's mother-in-law was her best friend. Moses and Joshua combined abilities and talents and caused a nation to be delivered. Peter and John are linked together as though they were one. Jesus needed friends. He called not one or two but twelve to be his friends. (Mark 3:14 RSV) Paul and Barnabas were inseparable. Paul wrote Timothy:

> How I thank God for you, Timothy. I pray for you every day, and many times during the long nights I beg my God tto bless you richly. How I long to see you again. How happy I would be, for I remember your tears as we left each other. (2 Tim. 1:3, 4 LB)

Jesus retreated to the home of his friend Lazarus when he needed to get away. There he kicked off his sandals and slept in a bed—a rarity for him. Martha laundered his dusty robe and served up a home-cooked meal.

Who can be a pastor's friend? Sometimes another pastor, but this has its limitations. First, a pastor knows the demands on his colleagues and he is reluctant to impose on them. Second, a clergyman needs perspective outside the clerical framework; someone within his parish who would know its specific needs and objectives and be able to give sound advice. Third, a pastor needs a friend for recreation, someone to work out with him in a gym or on a tennis court, who will help to get his mind completely off shop and let him be a plain ordinary man.

Who is that person? Who will be a pastor's friend? When other pastors are too pressured, when he needs an outside perspective, or someone to participate in recreational activity—that friend must be a layman, that rare breed, *a pastor's layman!*

He doesn't happen overnight. There is no formula. There is a beginning, a growing awareness that they understand one another. The friendship may start in casual conversation or in a discussion of the layman's personal problem. The pastor may find himself moving from listener to speaker with this man who is on the same wavelength, who knows how to empathize. The friend will make time to be with him. He begins to see a human being like himself. Over a period of time he demonstrates trustworthiness. He shares with his pastor-friend his faith and vision for his church. If there is a disturbance in the fellowship he feels the pastor should know about it. Together they pray, talk, and decide how to handle it. The friendship grows. The layman, though he respects the office of his pastor, lets him come down off the pedestal and be a man. A friend!

The pastor realizes he has found a rich treasure, that he doesn't have to play a role. He may slip up, make a mistake, be less than he is capable of being, but he knows that with this man he will not receive the "look what our pastor did or didn't do" treatment. Instead, the understanding of this pastor's layman will help him get things together again. The pastor may find release from a problem hindering his effectiveness. Now he can pick up his tasks with renewed faith and energy.

THEY CRY, TOO!

The pastor's layman will become increasingly aware of his pastor's needs. He will take hold in areas that are delicate but need firm attention.

An article appeared in a national religious publication that every minister must have found heartwarming. Every layman and laywoman in the world should read it. Appropriately it was titled "The Care and Feeding of Shepherds." Here is part of it:

> . . . With an unmistakable call to serve as a committed layman, I found myself in a position to minister to the needs of spiritual shepherds. . . . Correcting this concept of co-workers in Christ freed me to minister to my pastor's needs as well as to be ministered to by him. This co-worker had been given specialized functions or gifts to be used in the Body of Christ, just as the Lord had given some to me. . . . I realized that this co-worker was also a co-struggler. His condition of redeemed sinner was no different than mine. Both of us stood before the grace of God—trying, failing, sometimes succeeding in being faithful to our calling. This realization enabled me to treat him as a fellow human being, rather than a "house Christian" to be called upon to say grace at special functions.

> Accepting my pastor as a fellow struggler meant that I tried to treat him the way I wanted him to treat me. . . . I did not expect him to be more than I was willing to be myself. Here are some of the forms my ministry to him took:

> Inviting him to play tennis, or to sit around and talk;

Believing in him, his potential, his promise, and thanking God for what He has done and is going to do in the pastor's life;

Insisting that he spend times of rest and vacation with his family and not members of the congregation;

Listening to him and meeting him where he is by extending myself as I really am, not as I want him to think I am;

Realizing that he has hundreds of names to remember when he stumbles over mine;

Being aware that there are moments when he needs the truth, not tact, the truth spoken in love, not hostility, and motivated by his need, not by my insecurities;

Realize that the congregation did not hire his wife and children. She does not have to be an officer of any group or even a member of it. She does not have to teach Sunday School or sing in the choir, just because she is the pastor's wife.

Treat their children as I treat the other children in the congregation;

Honor the privacy of their personal lives.

Pray for them always.[1]

Mr. Cliff Stabler, the author, includes 'Trying to sense his needs before they become pressing." This is one of the delicate areas referred to above, the pastor's financial situation. The pastor's layman sees to it that the proper board or committee is informed about salary raises with built-in inflationary provisions, health insurance, a good retirement plan, and a well-kept, cheerful parsonage or manse.

Another delicate area is that of an incompetent, disloyal, or divisive staff member. The senior minister in far too many denominations must sit back and wait and wait—and wait until something happens to remove this individual. A trusted, competent layman can pick up the ball and see that something is done as quickly as possible. One wonders why this kind of sloppiness is tolerated in the greatest business of all—the business of helping people to grow spiritually. During our years of traveling, we met pastors of the churches we served who waited it out—a waste of precious time and energy that could never be recouped. Some denominations have the necessary provisions for taking care of such situations. Those who don't need to review their policies in this area.

A wise pastor's layman can, within the framework of the existing organization, help relieve the pastor and the church of an unproductive staff member firmly, kindly, sensibly, and with a minimum of disruption in the life of the church.

A pastor's layman is not a "yes" man. This is the strength of the friendship. He does not always agree with the pastor. He evaluates and contemplates thoughtfully and prayerfully the broader outlook as a layman and as a committed "minister" to *his* friend. When his pastor asks his advice he knows he is asking a trusted man who has weighed the many possible ramifications and consequences of a given course of action. The layman sees the pastor's point of view as he grows in knowledge about him, while keeping a layman's perspective.

A pastor can be assured, after consulting with his friend, that what is presented to the proper committees and boards has been properly apprized and has a sound knowledgeable basis. When a decision is reached, this key layman has an inestimable influence in bringing about a good decision because he is highly respected, thoughtful, fair, and can play "devil's advocate" to present all points of view.

A pastor's layman is totally committed to his Lord, his church, and his pastor, and it bears repetition: a good pastor's layman knows the difference between commitment and agreement! The difference between *principle* and *prejudice!*

Much is being said about prejudice as a major root cause of societal problems. Sociologists, students, and contemporary philosophers preach that society adhere to principle rather than to prejudice. To be completely without prejudice is totally impossible, but ridding ourselves of unfounded prejudice is a worthy goal. Although some might expect Christ's church on earth to be perfect, and therefore be the logical institution to pursue principle, it is plagued by too many of its constituents who do not know the difference. First, let's consult the dictionary:

> Principle: [as it relates here] a source or origin; a fundamental truth; an ultimate basis or cause; primary or basic law, doctrine or the like.[2]

> Prejudice: preconceived judgment or opinion; unreasonable predilection or grounds before sufficient knowledge.[3]

Here is how it might apply to members of a church congregation who do not know how to differentiate between them. A Christian person of principle believes basically that Christ is his Savior and Lord and that his personal responsibility and that of his church is to minister to each other and to those outside the fellowship of believers. Much of this is principle based on Christ's commandment, "Go and make disciples in all the nations . . . and then teach these new disciples to obey all the commands I have given you." (Matt. 28:19, 20 LB)

On this principle rests the Christian's raison d'être, the reason for being. It may involve a thousand different ways of obeying Jesus' command, but *this is why we are!* It means "becoming all things to all men in order to bring some to Christ." When something gets in the way of this principle, often it is because of tradition, custom, or unwillingness to change, which results in prejudice.

Whether or not church people will accept it, change is taking place in the church as much as in other places. But some diehards hang onto the concept of man-made forms and habits, which they view as sacrosanct. Here are some illustrations involving principle and prejudice that are common in the church:

> *Prejudice:* Eleven o'clock on Sunday morning is the only time to worship God. This is pure tradition. It was instituted when our country was a rural society. People were up at the crack of dawn, did the chores, ate a hearty breakfast, bathed and dressed in "Sunday-go-to-meetin' " clothes, hitched up the horse and buggy, and got to church about eleven o'clock on the "Lord's day."
>
> *Principle:* We can worship God at any time and should. The first Christians, who had to go underground, worshipped whenever they could secretly get together. Sunday was named after Sol, the ancient heathen god. It was adopted as a Christian day of worship because it was the first day of the week, thought to be our Lord's day of Resurrection. There is a little tourist resort town in

Wisconsin that is dependent upon tourism as its primary source of income. Some of the churches in this little town hold their worship service Thursday evening. The issue is not the time of worship, but the fact that we worship together.

Prejudice: Some lay people object to young people with long hair and sandaled feet coming into the church building to worship. (They would then have to refuse Jesus' entrance in his native clothing.)

Principle: It is true that Paul stresses that everything be done in an orderly fashion. Disruption by these people might be cause for alarm. However, I have yet to hear about these young people acting disrespectfully in church. On the contrary, they are deeply sincere, attentive, and eager to hear the words of their Jesus. Have we made too much of Sunday-best clothing? In those early days, people were lucky to have one Sunday-best outfit, not dozens. How many people are excluded from church because of overindulgence in an expensive variety of clothing?

Principle: The pastors and boards of churches propose new things to minister to changing times and needs. They do not believe in the horse-and-buggy approach to God. We should do his work with the most up-to-date methods available. Businesses go bankrupt if they don't update. Many churches are bankrupt because of people who hold them back. Visionaries believe "we can give it a try." Our purpose is to bring people to Christ in any way we can get the message across, as did the Apostle Paul.

> *Prejudice:* People resist change. Some of the traditionalists think anything new is too drastic. They resist because "it's never been done that way before." Another phrase that does not belong in the living, vital Body of the Church.

The growing Christian will learn the difference between *principle* and *prejudice!*

A pastor of a church came up with what he thought was a fine program. He wanted to try it out for size, so he called on one of several trusted pastor's laymen. As he aired his plan, the man listened carefully, nodded thoughtfully, made some comments, and pondered its possibilities. When the pastor finished presenting his proposal, this honest pastor's friend said, "Jim, that is one of the best ideas I have heard. It could be of great value to our church, *but*, it wouldn't be wise to do it now! You might win the battle and lose the war. A year from now I think it will work. But, if you want to go ahead with it now, I will support you 100 percent!" This layman, upon whom the pastor had come to depend with increasing assuredness, was right. The program was delayed for a year and, when it was implemented, was enthusiastically supported by all, and was a success.

Notice! This layman did not stomp and holler and threaten to subvert if he did not like the idea. He agreed that the program was good, but the timing was not right. How different from the actions of those who think only in terms of the immediate and of their personal prejudices. The difference between *principle* and *prejudice!* Note, too, that this layman made it clear that, despite a difference of opinion, he would support, not subvert, the efforts of his friend-pastor *whenever* the pastor wanted to put the plan into action.

Contrast that with another type of layman (thank goodness these are few). He hears about a proposal with which he does not agree. It may come from his pastor, from a board, or through hearsay. He hears what he wants to hear. Immediately his fists go up. He starts his own uninformed rumor with "Do you know what they are doing to our church? We can't let them do that!"

He sees himself as defender, crusader, hero, carrying invisible sword, shield, and helmet. He charges! Misinformed, mind closed, driven! By blind emotional prejudice—not principle!

He is to be pitied, but before pity sets in the satanic forces go to work through him. He goes on a rampage and leaves in his wake a path of destruction worse than any Hurricane Hilda or Hannah! Satan has loosed irretrievable powers through this man, unsettling many peaceful people. He is used by the Adversary to paralyze the mission of the Body of Christ: that of bringing food to the spiritually hungry, not taking up sword and shield to mislead and confuse them.

In our varied friendships with pastors, we discovered that most of them have laymen and women like that in their churches. What a waste! But I have yet to meet a pastor, a man sent by God, who does not have compassion for them. These men of God will forgive, excuse, and defend those few with the Spirit of Christ personified. "This man, or woman has problems, and he or she needs our love." Meek? Mild? Afraid? Defensive? Weak? Indecisive? No! A thousand times no! They are men sent by God to show his love: to the strong, the weak, the scared, the desperate, the lonely—even to those who refuse his love.

A layman, when informed about this study, wrote the following letter:

> Some months ago I was asked to speak to a group of laymen. I was supposed to speak about the love of Christ which I tried to share to the best of my ability.

Somehow I knew, it wasn't enough. There was something else I needed to say, and I couldn't put my finger on it.

I am a builder-contractor. Last year my church asked me to build an education building for the church, which we sorely needed. The new building was to be an extension of the existing structure.

The project went on for four months, and involved close contact with many aspects of church life of which I was completely unaware. It involved directly the pastor's office. What I learned during these four months of daily contact with the pastor, his staff and secretary, have made me a new layman. Never before did I realize just what these people carry on their shoulders.

As time went on I became a fixture, and people who happened in, began to demand certain things from me. Where was the pastor? Why was he not in his office? Why didn't he attend to such and such? When in fact the man was dashing from office, to counselling, to hospital, to mortuary, to board luncheons and visits to homes in trouble. The telephone never stopped: Worse than in my own office! People came to that little office by droves. People discouraged, unhappy, sorrowing, irate, seeking hope, in need of counselling. Repairmen, office supply people, happy people, sad people, dissatisfied people, Pastor-you-should-know-this people (I know, because they had no inhibitions about telling me), etc., etc.

Because of that four month experience I am absolutely convinced, even though other professions, including mine, have many pressures on them, the pastor's profession is IMPOSSIBLE to carry out fully and completely!

I found my message for the laymen. This is what I told them:

"If you have a pastor who loves you and can tell you about God's love, thank God for that!

"If you have a pastor who is a 'good' preacher and has any other pastoral talents thank God and praise Him for His blessings.

"If you have a pastor who is a 'great' preacher, and can administrate, comfort the sick, the grieving, and minister to the general needs of most of the people in the church (and this is by far most of the pastors in our country). *Thank God, praising Him, and fall on your knees before Him for having sent you such a man!"*

Your pastor needs and wants friends from the entire church. Often church members wait for the pastor to make friends with them, even when he is new to his parish. He seems to be the epitome of confidence and aggressiveness from the pulpit, but inwardly he may be quite the opposite. He can't say to a member, "Would you please be my friend?" He may want to but, like you, may be afraid of rejection. Take the examples of several different couples in a church, which one of our pastor friends experienced:

A young man and his wife were members of a church for a number of years before the new pastor was called to serve. Before long they let it be known that they could not get to know him because "he was too busy for them"—resting comfortably in that rusty routine. When the pastor discovered this kind of contrived rejection, he decided to remedy the situation.

He tried in every way that seemed natural to reach out to them. They conversed over coffee in Sunday school classes and after church on Sunday mornings, though the pastor needed quiet and privacy to prepare himself for preaching.

The cover-up, "he doesn't have time for us," continued. The pastor's wife invited them in on Sunday nights after four teaching and preaching services, for specially prepared suppers. The pastor called the man repeatedly for luncheon appointments and other howdies by phone, receiving little response. That pastor is still waiting for the storybook ending.

This is the unique mystique of Christ's church and of the "man sent by God," who shepherds that church. It shows the limitless love of God working through the limited love of his man, who is infused with unfathomable love. Isn't it too bad that some "believers" expect God's man to have limitless love for them, when it is all right for them to withhold theirs. If that pastor is still waiting for a little love from that couple, and if it finally comes, he will praise God for it. Your minister may cry, too, but he is a *big* man!

Let me relate a story that has a "storybook ending":

A young couple brought sheer joy to the man sent by God who was to become their pastor—this man hungry for friendship and some lighthearted fellowship. They moved into the community he served. They were young Christians, full of vitality and adventure. They didn't waste any time looking for a church home. Though there were loads of boxes to be unpacked, they started out on their first Sunday in town to look for spiritual fulfillment. They didn't use the well-worn phrase, "We're looking for a church home," too long. Too many Christians use this albatross excuse to duck their commitment to their former church covenant and vows. Within the first month these people joined a church.

The following week the pastor, his wife, and four children were invited to that home for dinner, with unpacked boxes serving as chairs. What a time that was. A beautiful friendship started. Creative talk ensued on books, music, art. Helpful ideas about the church from which they came were pursued in a positive way. The friendship has continued to grow through the years, though their career took them to another community.

A pastor's son told his father, "Dad, I don't know what God wants me to do with my life. It may or may not be the ministry. If it isn't the ministry, I have decided to be the very best pastor's friend and lay man I know how to be. Because being a preacher's kid I have seen how much these men mean to you. Maybe some day I can mean that to my pastor."

Checklist

_____ You may be the person God wants for your pastor's layman. The only requirement is empathy. Let him know that with you he can be himself and that you accept his humanness. Develop sensitivity to his needs. You may discover your spiritual gift and ministry.

_____ If you do not feel that you are that special layman, you can still be a very special friend. You can provide recreation and diversion—something every minister desperately needs.

_____ If you are aware of something your minister should know about—maybe a family need, a church need; maybe some unfounded rumor or staff tension, tell your pastor about it. He will appreciate your concern, and it could avert serious difficulties.

_____ A beautiful way to express friendship is to honor your pastor's need for privacy and help others to heed it. The car he drives, how he spends his vacation, the color of his wife's hair, and the cut or uncut grass—these are his personal affairs.

_____ If you sense discouragement or weariness, tell him something positive that has happened in your life, or in the life of someone you know, because of his ministry. You may be God's messenger to him for that day and make it brighter.

_____ If you prefer a casual relationship with your pastor, fine. However, allow him and his family to have close friends without disapproving. Think of how you would react if your career or job required that you cancel all close friendships!

_____ Etiquette involves courtesy. Courtesy involves kindness. Be kind to your pastor. He needs friends, too!

6

Questions about
HIS BANK ACCOUNT

Why should anyone be concerned about the minister's bank account? Balancing the budget is becoming more time consuming and wellnigh impossible. Inflation, devaluation, and shortages have hit our country in proportions we did not dream possible. There may be those who think they have enough financial difficulties of their own without worrying about anyone else's economic status, least of all the pastor's. As in the past, there is great concern about our country's financial problems. At the same time there is, as in the past, a higher law at work—the law of *divine mathematics.*

This law was stated and practiced for eighty-three years by a completely human saint, my father-in-law, who founded and supervised the Rescue Mission in Oakland, California, for nearly sixty years. His income was $85 a month during the depression and stayed that way during more prosperous years. It was hardly what might be referred to as a salary. But Daddy Lavender believed with a passion in God providing and honoring his meager tithe. If he saw a need that was immediate among his clients on skid row, the tithe was forgotten as he gave more.

During World War II he bought an old house—with divine mathematics—fixed it up mostly by himself, and asked for volunteers to serve coffee and sandwiches and to witness to Christ's love for lonely directionless servicemen. He and his volunteers ministered to two million, all because of a man's unshakable conviction that, if everybody gives something out of their nothing, it is miraculously multiplied.

Divine mathematics does work for everyone who tries it! It has to, because 95 percent of the clergymen ministering to the spiritual well-being of our country are grossly underpaid. And, as mentioned earlier, the mind-set of parishioners is to expect the pastor to live a hand-to-mouth existence.

The respect a parish has for its minister can mean the difference between a dynamic or a defeated church leadership. The willingness or unwillingness of a congregation to meet adequately its pastor's physical needs, affects how a pastor feels about his ministry and his sense of worth. The church members' sense of stewardship is transmitted through him —self-respect and appreciation—or quite the opposite.

Distressingly, the oft-repeated phrase, "Where your treasure is, there will your heart be also," (Matt. 6:21 RSV) continues to be in stiff competition with the old saw, still in the consciousness of a majority of church members, "Lord, you keep him humble—we'll keep him poor." An area minister (a pastor to pastors) observes:

> A contributing factor in the failure of many pastors has been the worry over money to care for himself and his family. A man with such worries will find it hard to serve his church without that worry showing through. In forty years of observing ministers I have known just two wealthy men among them. Both of these had married wealthy women.[1]

As you read the statement about those two wealthy pastors, what was your reaction? Wealthy pastors? They are not supposed to be! That was my reaction, too, because that's the opposite of everything I've been taught to believe about ministers and money. When lay persons are successful financially, people are proud to have them in their church. A pastor would not dare be successful financially—a first class example of a double standard.

As a child, some attitudes fixed themselves all too indelibly in my mind. I witnessed in a small midwestern town the shabby treatment of a distinguished educated gentleman in our little church. He was our pastor. What a man of his ability and background was doing in this tiny community was to me a wonder. I adored him, and he loved the kids, much to the chagrin of the old pillars. He was provided with free housing, through the generosity of an elderly couple who gave what they had—two dark, dingy upstairs bedrooms converted into an "apartment," kerosene stove and all. If there was anything left over after the church bills were paid out of the offerings, the pastor received a "salary."

He had a daughter who was my closest friend. She was a beautiful child with long blonde curls, named Evangeline. I spent a lot of time with her and occasionally shared a family meal. I remember more than once her mother trying to do something with a slimy chicken or a tough, strong-tasting leg of mutton to put meat on the table, "donated" by a church member.

In Sunday school we were taught about the Old Testament concept of bringing firstfruits to the Old Testament ministers called priests. I never could quite figure out the meaning of firstfruits, except that I knew it was a very special offering to the Lord. When we tried to eat the tough mutton at the preacher's apartment, I was quite sure this was not firstfruits.

THEY CRY, TOO!

It was "lastfruits" somebody else wouldn't eat. I remember, too, it was an offering not "without spot or blemish."

I do remember, though, with kindness, a few dear folks who were compassionate believers and did bear their firstfruits. My mother was one of them. We kids beat many a path up those backstairs to that attic apartment with freshly butchered roasted chicken, fresh vegetables or some of the best meat on butchering day. Sometimes momma would deliberately cut out one piece of fresh, handwhipped angel food cake and take it over with a "we couldn't eat it all, the chickens laid real good this week," so it would be easier for the lady of the manse to accept. However, I noticed the tears of this genteel foreign-born lady who had dedicated her life, along with her husband, to the ministry. At the tender age of five I often wondered what she was thinking.

Many reading this will recall those years of depression, when everyone struggled to have enough to eat and clothes to wear. However, in comparison with the frugal ghetto existence of this minister's family, the homes and tables of the members of his church were kingly.

Lest one think this an exaggerated experience in the mind of an impressionable child, another little rural church comes to mind today. It is located in the heart of the rich San Joaquin valley of California. It is surrounded by thousands of acres of rich vineyards. Its parish is comprised of huge farm owners, who produce grapes for the booming wine industry. They live in large new ranch homes, with the latest conveniences, the latest farm equipment, with several trucks and family cars. To date, they owe their pastor at least eight months' salary. His wife must work to support the family. If church utility bills are not paid he and his wife pay them.

Some of these church members do not mind telling visitors that out of the last five pastors to serve their church, two had had heart attacks (one fatal), one had developed ulcers, one had a complete breakdown, and another left in despair. When some of these men sent by God tried new things to bring about new vitality, most old-timers objected. When nothing new was happening, they complained. The present pastor continues to love and minister to people, whether for and against him. When asked why there is a "for and against group," there is no rational answer. One person offered: "It's always been that way." What a trademark by which to become known in a church of Christ, put here to be a light to the world. The light in that church can be no more than a flicker.

The clerical survey, to which nearly forty major denominations responded, revealed some startling information about pastors' salaries. A middle-to-low income median average prevails, but in one instance, there is a sudden jump to a salary figure double the average. It could mean either that someone is overpaid or that at last the church is beginning to take Paul seriously. "Pastors who do their work well should be paid well." (1 Tim. 5:17 LB) It is the salary quoted by the Jewish Conference of Rabbis (housing and retirement are additional benefits). According to the rabbi who responded to the survey this was considered a "moderate" salary.

It is thought-provoking that these people still look for their messiah. Christians believe their Messiah has come. They, of all people, should be most joyous and generous. If giving is an indication of one's faith, and Jesus thought it was, whose faith is the greater?

In Jerusalem, the early Christians brought everything they owned and shared it. These were Jewish Christians. They were raised in the concept of the firstfruits and the tithe and did not discard that law because they became followers of Christ. As many times as I have read the story of Pentecost, I did not discover something of great significance about that event until recent study.

The Holy Spirit was given to Jews of the Dispersion, who had come to Jerusalem to celebrate two feasts, the Feast of Firstfruits, "When you arrive in the land I will give you, and reap your first harvest, bring the first sheaf of the harvest" (Lev. 23:9 LB), and the Feast of Pentecost, "Fifty days later you shall bring to the Lord an offering of a sample of the new grain." (Lev. 23:15 LB) These first Hebrew Christians came not empty-handed, not to receive, but to give. Little did they know what was in store for them when that marvelous outpouring happened! What a return on their investment!

> All the tithe of the land, whether of the seed of the land or of the fruit of the trees, is the Lord's; it is holy to the Lord. If a man wishes to redeem any of his tithe [i.e., borrow from it], he shall add a fifth to it [i.e., interest]. And all the tithe of herds and flocks, every tenth animal of all that pass under the herdsman's staff shall be holy to the Lord. (Lev. 27:30–32 RSV)

Translated into today's language this reads: "Cattlemen, agriculturalists, farmers, ranchers, oilmen, doctors, lawyers, laborers, teachers, bus drivers, postmen—give one-tenth of what you earn!"

> Bring all the tithes into the storehouse. . . . If you do, I will open up the windows of heaven for you and pour out a blessing so great you won't have room enough to take it. (Mal. 3:10 LB)

> If you love me, you will keep my commandments. (John 14:15 RSV)

> Think not that I have come to abolish the law and the prophets; I have come not to abolish them but to fulfill them. (Matt. 5:17 RSV)

When, in the development of the Christian church, was the principle of the tithe put aside and ignored? When the Gentiles became Christians? They were the affluent of that day. Certainly not the Jews, under the oppresive, greedy heel of Rome.

One minister reported, "Boy, our church is in great shape! We're going to get a new paint job in the sanctuary. We've been promised two new youth centers. Our education building will be remodeled. My study will be painted, and I think I will get a new desk so I don't have to keep nailing up the old one."

Naturally his friends were curious about the big windfall to his church. Someone asked, "Where is all this money coming from?"

"Oh," replied the minister, "when one of our men gets his big promotion, when and if the wheat crop comes through in the fall, when the real-estate dealer has some good deals, when Pete's four kids are through college, and Henry's well comes in."

How many Christians are missing the joy of giving the mite, while they wait to do something big? For most, that day never comes.

It is important in this chapter to bring into perspective pastoral pay as it relates to other occupations and professions.

To gain information, experts in various professions and occupations were consulted. Research in libraries brought to light helpful documents. The clerical questionnaire mentioned earlier included a segment about pastors' finances. A pamphlet issued by the U.S. Department of Labor, Bureau of Labor Statistics, provided an excellent study. It presented a list of occupations, median annual earnings, and median educational backgrounds—separate ones for men and women. It was based on the latest census. The lists were numbered, with number one as the highest-paid occupation, and the last number the lowest-paid occupation.

Out of 432 occupations listed, clergymen ranked number 316. Clergywomen ranked 317, their salaries half that of their male counterparts. Clergy rank with the lowest-paying occupations and with unskilled labor—library attendants, teacher aides, waiters and waitresses, cooks, farm laborers, and file clerks. Though they rank next to the bottom economically, educationally they rank with the ten top earning occupations—lawyers, physicians, dentists, judges, college professors, scientists, engineers and managers. Most of the 107 below their earning rank did not graduate from high school, while many did not go beyond the eighth grade.[2]

What is more disturbing is that the clergy showed the lowest percentage of salary increase among their professional peers in a ten-year period. Actual clergy salaries at the *end* of this ten-year period are still less than those most professionals included in the study earned at the *beginning* of the same ten-year period.

The generally low salary for the clergy is accompanied by a shocking lack of fringe benefits, taken for granted by most American workers. A large percentage of churches do not provide pension, health insurance, annuity plans, or life insurance coverage. Virtually none receive disability or dental insurance.

Pastors' professional expenses are modestly covered, if at all. A large number of those responding to a survey financed by the Ministers Life and Casualty Union, subsidized their own automobile expenses. Many pastors personally pay expenses for their professional development, for continuing education, and for the books, religious periodicals, and theological volumes necessary for reference in their work.

How do clergy feel about this? From the survey mentioned above there is this observation:

> Few clergy enter the ministry in order to make money. Indeed, most pastors are quite satisfied with

their work! Those seeking a change that would involve leaving the parish ministry were only four percent of the total! But it is true that most of the dissatisfaction centers around the problem of money. As one man commented:

"I feel that the ministry is one of the most important activities which we are called upon to provide. . . . Unfortunately, many of us are so financially strapped and in debt that we cannot afford to carry out an effective or dynamic ministry—making use of our gifts and skills and meeting the widest range of our peoples' needs."[3]

To alleviate some of the financial pressures, ministers are having to find other ways of earning income:

1. Ministers must resort to secular employment. Five times as many ministers hold two or more jobs as those in the regular labor force.

2. Ministers are serving two or more congregations. Though the churches are small, each is a complete entity, and a pastor cannot serve up half a ministry. Therefore, demands upon his time and energies are more than double.

3. Wives must go to work. 42 percent of married women in the general population work, while 45 percent of clergymen's wives work. Two-thirds of these work out of economic necessity, while still expected to take an active part in church functions.

In the light of these bleak facts about an unpopular subject—what your minister is *paid*, not what he *earns*, it is hoped that the reader will begin to ask some questions:

How much dissatisfaction with pay can a minister be

expected to tolerate? Is it fair to let a minister, in debt because of a low salary, simply worry and become discouraged when no way is seen to get out of debt?

Should a pastor *have* to undertake secular employment as a way of meeting basic financial obligations?

Should a clergy wife *have* to take a job because her family cannot get along on her husband's pay?

How do these factors affect a pastor's morale, family life, or ability to perform an effective ministry?[4]

There is a notion still at large that should be laid to rest—the notion that people, whether they give or not, own their pastor. He was sent by God, and he belongs to him. He is responsible for doing his job well, but that does not make him an object to be possessed. When we buy a car, we do not own the chairman of the board. When we pay for the services of a doctor, lawyer, hairdresser, or milkman, we do not own them. We bought a service. Nor do we tell them how to perform the service in which they specialize and for which they are trained. However, this is what many do to their pastor. Minorities are clamoring to be freed, and are using acceptable, or unacceptable methods to achieve this. Clergymen, though a sizable minority, will not resort to overt behavior. They believe that the goodness of God's people will prevail and release them from being owned.

The Yearbook of American and Canadian Churches found that:

An increase in income for the pastor is translated into his giving more money to the

church. Conversely, an increase in income for
the laity means support for many other things
than merely a gift to the church.[5]

Some readers might argue that most churches are small,
having from 50 to 300 members, and cannot pay their pastor
as they would like. I will argue back that it is possible. The
U.S. Labor Department issues a report on median earnings
periodically. Ten percent of those reported earnings would
give even the smallest congregation an impressive budget. It
would allow for a respectable salary, and there would be
enough left for a staff helper. A tithing church will be a
growing church. Its vitality will be noticed and people will
want to join that kind of fellowship, and bring in more income.

Though many people do give generously, the church is
suffering because it is not receiving its rightful share. Much of
the giving done by its members goes to many agencies
outside the church. This proliferation of monies is becoming
a major problem for the churches of our country. To some
degree, this has been going on for many years. But religion
has become big business, involving millions of dollars. Its
lure is the glamorous, the spectacular, and it bombards us on
all sides.

"I hear and see so many appeals for radio and television
programs, crusades, seminars, institutes, orphanages, religious clubs, study fellowships, and youth organizations.
They are so wonderful I would like to give to all of them. But
I don't know which ones to support."

This is the reaction of individuals who feel they should
help support such causes. On the surface, all appear to be
worthwhile. Therefore it is important that one consider carefully the cause to which one would like to give financial aid.

This poses a dilemma, and it should be dealt with as
thoughtfully as any other major decision. Not only is it

important to be generous stewards, it is equally important to be wise stewards. God has made you executor of his estate, and he wants you to use your part wisely, and to give back to him his part. As in the parable of the talents, i.e., money, the master was most pleased with the man who multiplied his portion not five but ten times. I believe the lesson in that parable teaches more about the wisdom of giving than about the amount given. That gift you give back to him should be utilized in the most productive way possible.

To give wisely means to be careful about giving on impulse, as the result of a highly emotional appeal. There should be a carefully worked out plan of giving. The basis on which to build is the tithe or one-tenth of all income. Giving beyond that is an offering. Church members should always regard their church as their first responsibility. That is the organization that utilizes it in the most productive way possible. What does not occur to people who bypass that responsibility, is that *without the church all of these other organizations would not and could not exist.* Because of the church they came into being, and because of the support of the church they continue to exist.

Probably as high as 95 percent of outside agencies' support comes from people who belong to churches. Church members' giving is the church's primary means of support, since these are the people interested in propagating the message of Christ. If Christian people give little or nothing to their church and give instead to other "worthwhile causes," they may themselves suffer spiritually. With the growing list of independent religious organizations outside the church vying for funds, it is possible that the church will become ineffective and neutralized—and that this increasing fragmentation of members' giving may result in the demise of many small churches.

Can you imagine what the congregation would think about seeing their pastor in a new suit every Sunday? Or if the choir sang in different, specially designed costumes every week? Or if the church obtained the services of the highest-paid musical arrangers and orchestras for every worship service? It doesn't take much to predict the reaction of a congregation to such expenditures. There would be no need to take up an offering. The offering plates would probably be returned empty. Yet thousands of church members send money to organizations that spend hundreds of thousands of dollars in the ways described above. Your own church and its outreach ministries could operate for a year on the budget required for one weekly television program.

There is another fact that most people who give to outside causes may not know. They may intend to give just once. However, when a letter with a gift is received, the donor's name is placed on a mailing list permanently. That person will continue to receive appeals by mail forever. In addition, after the first contribution, the mailbox suddenly comes alive with fund appeals from a rash of sources. The giver may well wonder from whence comes this sudden popularity. His or her name, along with thousands of others, is put on a mailing list, which in turn becomes a marketable item. Your name is being sold and you may not know about it—nor do you have any control over it. There are businesses that exist solely for the purpose of selling mailing lists to political, charitable, educational, religious, and sales organizations.

There is the story of a fellow named Jim Brown, who was very proud of his alma mater. Naturally, over the years he had received many a fund appeal from his school. Too many, he finally decided. One, in particular, didn't set too well. So he resealed the envelope, printed "deceased" on it, and mailed it back. That stopped the appeals—for three months. To his amazement he then received another appeal addressed to the "Estate of Jim Brown."

Something else to be considered is how much of your contribution goes directly to the fund itself. A large percentage is spent on promotion, advertising, air time, printing, mailing costs, administration, salaries, and travel expenses for representatives who promote the appeals for funds.

One other thing should be carefully weighed when you consider giving to an agency outside your church. As a church member, a believer, a Christian, on whom can you call in time of personal need, family crisis, illiness, death, or other tragedy? *Your church.* A Christian friend, a caring elder or deacon, and, more often, your pastor, who is only a telephone call away at any hour of the day or night, will come at once to help.

Isn't giving the Lord's money to your own church practical, sensible, and wise stewardship?

Fair consideration must be given to long-established reputable organizations, crusades, and ministries that have proven their effectiveness and operated on the highest principles. Their format is simple, and they avoid ostentatious productions. After one's first responsibility—to one's church—has been fulfilled, by testing God's *divine mathematics*, there will be plenty left to contribute to those organizations that can be trusted to use God's money carefully and not misuse your good name.

A farmer who plants just a few seeds will get only a small crop, but if he plants much, he will reap much. . . . God is able to make it up to you by giving you everything you need and more, so that not only will there be enough for your own church's needs, but plenty left over to give joyfully to others." (2 Cor. 9:6, 8 LB)

Again, I think of Daddy Lavender, who used to take his little son out for a walk in the beautiful hills of the San

Francisco Bay area and point out: "Son, see those beautiful hills there, those green forests, the cattle grazing, that great ocean and all those ships? We're rich, son, because our Father owns all of these! We're rich because God is our Father. Everything we think we own, belongs to him. Never forget that!" This faithful man—poor, very poor by all our standards, thought he was rich!

Divine mathematics! Was he kidding himself? If so, he had it incredibly all put together. He was way ahead of his time. Young people today think they are doing something new and different by eschewing material things while looking for icks, trying to find God through drugs, going back to nature, and, praise the Lord, many finding Christ. But Daddy Lavender knew he was rich in his God nearly a century ago. There are thousands of such dedicated ministers today giving everything they have in time, effort, and money, who are the real Jesus people. And I say that with reverence. Are they to be short-changed because of their commitment?

Checklist

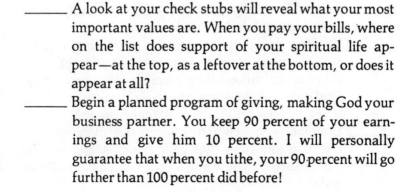

_____ A look at your check stubs will reveal what your most important values are. When you pay your bills, where on the list does support of your spiritual life appear—at the top, as a leftover at the bottom, or does it appear at all?

_____ Begin a planned program of giving, making God your business partner. You keep 90 percent of your earnings and give him 10 percent. I will personally guarantee that when you tithe, your 90 percent will go further than 100 percent did before!

_____ Educate your children in giving. Don't let them grow up with a nickel-and-dime concept of God, when they spend many more times that on the Saturday matinee.

_____ Compare the salaries of your pastor with other professional people with similar responsibilities and training, i.e., physicians, psychiatrists, lawyers, and school principals. Begin to bring his salary in line with these.

_____ Church leaders should do something about a built-in cost-of-living clause and fringe benefits for their pastors. Education, tenure, experience, responsibilities, and work hours, all should be considered.

_____ Your pastor should not have to ask for a raise. It is extremely embarrassing for him and for the church when he is not able to pay his bills.

_____ If your church provides a home for the pastor, see what needs to be done to make it comfortable and cheerful. Maybe it needs remodeling, or maybe you need a new parsonage.

_____ If there is a church-owned home, it could be to the pastor's disadvantage if living in it is considered part of his salary. The pastor is paying for the home, while the church retains possession. Churches are beginning to remedy this by loaning interest-free money to the pastor to purchase his own home.

_____ If, after giving your tithe to your first responsibility—your church—you want to give to some other organization, shop carefully before you buy. Find out everything you can about that organization, to see if God is getting the most for his money.

_____ Examine your church budget for missions and outreach ministries that your church supports. You will be surprised how much your church does with so little.

7
Questions about
HIS WIFE

Is your minister's wife expected to be an "assistant pastor"? In some ways, the challenges that confront her are even more demanding than those that face her husband. . . . In an age when more and more attention is being directed towards liberating women from traditionally confining roles, it seems appropriate to consider ways in which ministers' wives can be freed from obligations that are often unnecessary and frequently frustrating. . . .

The greatest contribution a minister's wife can make is to *be herself*, building on her own interests. . . . But if you really expect her to be an "assistant pastor," don't forget to pay her.[1]

Thus reads a nationwide advertisement.

Ministers' wives are very special people. They are sharp, educated, capable (in areas other than singing in the choir and teaching Sunday School), artistic, creative, and attractive. They are actively involved in community programs. They hold a variety of jobs that require intelligence and expertise. Their educational background is continually improving as they keep pace with that of their husbands'. A majority hold Bachelor of Arts degrees, thousands have their Masters, and many have Ph.Ds.

Though there is growing liberation from past expectations of this woman's role, there is much progress yet to be made. There are a number of areas in which she must still walk a fine line. One is in the area of friendships. She is wary of developing close relationships. If she misjudges and shares her deep feelings, it could lead to disaster. Coming from others, what is confided might produce a ripple. Coming from the pastor's wife, it could cause a tidal wave.

She limits herself to few friends and doesn't allow them to really get to know her. Realizing that her faults and weaknesses may not be accepted, she draws back for fear of discovery. In the midst of a busy, demanding life, she is lonely.

Ministers' wives become resentful when husbands are married to their profession. This they share with other professionals' wives. There is an added factor: She should not complain about doing God's work, regardless of how much it takes her husband from her. Thus, in addition to feeling hostile, she feels guilty.

There is another area in which this woman is restricted. It is theoretically the right and duty of every church member, but, in actuality, here she is persona non grata. Protestant churches are democratically structured and all members may participate in church business affairs. There is open discussion and all members may vote. While the pastor's wife may speak on an issue, it had better be under her breath if it differs from the consensus. Though she may have constructive insights within her frame of reference, she knows it is best to remain silent. In this regard she is a second class citizen in her congregation.

In practical matters, she dare not shout at the kids, in case the neighbors might hear. What does she do about the dog from across the street that tears up her shrubs? What if someone who knows her sees steak or cooking wine in her shopping cart at the market? She knows that Christians must be discreet in all things. Does that mean that routine things like the ones above may be carried out openly by others, but she must do them in secret? Every day of her life she faces this dilemma.

In a ministers' wives survey, in which forty-two out of fifty responded, one question was to express whatever was uppermost in their minds. Here are a few of their reactions:

My husband contends that one reason I get along well in our pastorates is the fact that I cannot play the piano or sing!

I miss being able to have special friends that we can just enjoy ourselves with, without feeling we are leaving others out.

We are programmed women. Programmed to behave like, act like, say yes to, whatever the church —especially the women—want us to do, according to their whims or personal preferences.

What really gets me is the mold into which the parishioners force the minister's wife.

To tell you the truth, I don't fit in. I prefer to be

alone. I'm very much an introvert and I feel I've
made a complete flop as a minister's wife. But my
husband insists he likes me the way I am, and that he
didn't marry me to be his assistant. His attitude is all
that makes life worth while.

The foregoing comments point up painfully that the wife of
a minister is still victim of an image from which she cannot
extricate herself (and there is no perceptible change on the
horizon): the minister's-wife image.

She, too, with her husband, is to be a moral leader in an
immoral world, which imposes this image as justification for
its acts. This is the world's image. This is not God's image. The
only image we should have is the image of Jesus, who walked
this earth as a human being, and his example leaves everyone
short of the mark.

Nowhere in Scripture do we find reference, teaching, advice, or standards for pastors' wives. We have no knowledge
of how many pastors and teachers in the early church were
married. The only one mentioned is Peter, whose mother-in-
law was healed by our Lord. (Luke 5:38, 39) Some scholars
suggest that Paul may have been married, since this was
required to be a member of the governing body, the
Sanhedrin. In the writings of Paul there is advice for pastors,
deacons, and elders. The major portions of his letters address
themselves to lay members. Several women are mentioned in
the New Testament church as followers of Christ, but there is
no mention of pastors' wives.

How did the pastor's wife acquire her present image? No
study about this has come to my attention. One might
speculate that as the church evolved to its present form, she,
along with her husband, was put on a pedestal—human, but,
hopefully, perfect. She was readily available to help out when
her husband could not attend to all the needs of his
congregation. In a basically rural society churches were simple

and small. Everything was done by the pastor, with the help of his wife, including keeping the church house clean. At the same time, she was expected to be an exemplary wife and mother and a good manager of all domestic responsibilities.

Though there still are many more small than large churches today, in an infinitely more complex society churches, too, have changed with the times. A farmer using a hand plow is rare in our culture. Yet the minister and his wife are, in many ways, regarded as though they were still in the hand plow era while being asked to serve a twentieth-century constituency.

With the exception of the president's wife (and she is free to pursue her individuality and favorite projects to her liking), no other wife is as constantly reminded about her spouse's career. People don't generally say, "May I present our electrician's wife, our dentist's wife, or our schoolteacher's wife." However, when a minister's wife is seen anyplace, or introduced, she is referred to as "our minister's wife." Why this kind of introduction is necessary remains a mystery. It may be intended as complimentary, but often it makes her, and the people to whom she is introduced, uncomfortable, especially outside of a church situation. "What am I supposed to do or say now?" is written on their faces, as out of the corner of their eyes they look for the nearest exit.

Two weeks before sending the final manuscript to the publisher, I placed a long-distance call to a well-known pastor about another matter. After telling me what I needed to know, he asked what I was doing. Since the finishing of this project was uppermost in my mind, I mentioned it, expected to thank him, and say good-bye. He immediately showed interest in the book and asked questions. I outlined what I was attempting to present and listed some of the subjects discussed. He commented here and there, and when I mentioned the title of this chapter he went into a verbal tailspin.

"You had better do a whole book on that subject. How

active have you been in the church? How active are you now? How do you deal with the "ought-to's" and "supposed to's"? Have you broken out?"

"Of what?" I asked, coming up for air in this unexpected rapid-fire volley.

"The mold! The image bit. Have you found out who you are? Your identity? Or are you still the minister's wife? How does your church take to your personal interests, your writing? I guess what I am trying to get at is, are you what your church expects you to be, or are you what God wants for you—to be your own person?"

With confrontation, but lovingly, he had opened up a Pandora's box that was crammed full. I found myself confiding unabashedly, not without some lumps in my throat, as this man sent by God ministered to me. Until that moment I had not known, nor had I been aware, that I, too, needed and deserved a pastor.

Ironically, one of your pastor's wife's greatest needs is for a pastor. She probably is not aware of it. Her husband may be the most wonderful pastor in the world. But he cannot be a pastor to his wife. She may think it possible, but he will always be, first, a husband. If he pleases her when she comes to him for counsel, she may regard him as a pastor. But if he feels compelled to give sound but hard-to-swallow advice, he suddenly will become a husband.

In reality, the wife of a pastor has no pastor. To whom should she go to confide feelings, hurts, and distresses? From whom can she get spiritual help? No one, unless she feels free to go to another pastor in the community. Because these wives know too well the demands upon a pastor's time, few, if any, will seek help there. Then too, they may feel ashamed and self-conscious about needing help. If so, these women need to deal with what is basically a form of pride.

A minister's wife should be *attractive*, but not too much so; have nice clothes, but not too nice (she will always be applauded for making her clothes); have a nice basic hair-do, but not too nice; be *friendly*, but not too friendly; be *aggressive* and greet everyone, especially visitors, but not too aggressive; *intelligent*, but not too intelligent; *educated*, but not too educated; *down-to-earth*, but not too much so; *capable*, but not too capable; *charming* but not too charming; and be *herself*—but not openly!

What she *can* be *too* is *spiritual* (depending on one's interpretation of the word), be her husband's faithful helpmeet (an archaic expression meaning what he can't get done in his work she should help him with), and *practical*. That she can *never* be, *too*. This highly approved *not too* is a virtue, because it involves being thrifty and a good manager with her husband's limited take-home pay. The biggest *not-too* she must be is *quiet* when her husband, children, or she, herself, is criticized.

A conversation with a pastor's wife comes to mind, which demonstrates the continued need for further understanding. This woman's husband had just retired from the active ministry. As a teen-ager, she herself had felt a call into some area of Christian service. (This is the exception rather than the rule. Most ministers' wives do not experience this per se. Their feeling of "call" comes when they decide to marry a man who feels that that is what he has been called to do.) She equipped herself well for her specialty in the field of evangelism and Christian education. She met her future husband, fell in love with him, and decided that was to be the form of her ministry for years to come. But her dream persisted.

While raising her family she had a most effective teaching ministry in her husband's churches. During their last pastorate she finally received her call in a vocational way. The church called her as director of Christian education and evange-lism—for pay!

"It was our happiest work in the ministry. I loved my work and was expected to do less on salary than I did for free before."

When both retired from that church she was asked how she viewed her many ministries. She responded, "I loved the pastorate, but especially the chance to express myself in my career those last years. As for leaving the role of pastor's wife—when I walked out the door of that church (and I attend there often now), I felt a great burden roll off me. I hadn't realized, loving the ministry as I do, the demands and the toll that it takes."

Lest anyone think this is sour grapes, or the groans of a fatigued senior citizen, this remarkable still-young (in her fifties) woman, who has since lost her husband, has accepted another challenge. She is teaching in a Christian college in a foreign country. She writes that it is marvelous to be "accepted on my own merit. Not as 'our pastor's wife.' "

Two summers ago, at a conference for pastors and their wives, one of the speakers was a psychologist. He spoke at length about the need for more constructive interaction between pastors and laity. He suggested ways in which they might be more open with each other. He saved some significant comments for pastors' wives. The gist of his remarks was that, although the stress factors of the pastor were way beyond those of any other professional occupation, the stress was greater for the wife. He suggested that this might be so because the pastor is there, at the "front," while she stands by and must quietly accept whatever comes his way, be it good, happy, unpleasant, mundane, wearying, or the emotional strain in gear-shifting discussed in an earlier chapter.

When we do have a chance to work with these women, the stress factors have caused damage to physical and emotional health almost beyond repair. The field of counseling pastors and pastors' wives is new. It is almost totally unexplored. They have no one to talk to, for fear their constituents will think less of them if they show human feelings. So they bottle it up. They smile at the person they would like to throw bricks at, who seems to be happiest when making trouble for their husbands. They say "Good morning" when they'd like to poke someone in the nose. I found that they find the handling of criticism about their husbands almost impossible. They would far rather take it upon themselves, or even their children, but let someone criticize their husband, who is giving of himself far more to everybody else than to them—they see red! And I don't blame them. It's much easier to be in there where it's at, than a bystander watching someone you love be unjustly—or justly for that matter, taken to task.

You can be sure that, for these women, that psychologist made a lot of brownie points.

Let some of these wives speak for themselves as they answer questions in the minister's wives survey mentioned earlier:

Question:
What are the things most rewarding and satisfying in the ministry?

Answers:
To see the transforming power of Christ.

People showing their love to us in tangible ways.

The fellowship of Christians.

Growing with people.

Helping those who need help.

Seeing unanswered prayer.

When teen-agers hang in there because of commitment to Christ!

Acceptance of us as people. We are not put on a pedestal.

Watching Christians begin to reach out to each other.

Question:

What are the things most disturbing and unrewarding?

Answers:

Isolation from close friendship.

Burden of feeling that all problems are the pastor's fault, and his responsibility.

Long hours away from home.

Pettiness.

Inability to ever get it all done.

We are supposed to be perfect.

Our children give up their father every night of the week. They should not have to give up their mother, too.

To see how church membership means so little to so many.

We are supposed to be puppets!

Being compared with the former minister's wife!

Separation of minister and people.

Some think my husband is a glorified errand boy.

The church does not keep up the parsonage.

Endless stupid meetings.

The first chapter of this book tells about several incidents that demonstrate the differences assigned to clergy and their families. Conversations with them bring this phenomenon sharply into focus. They express a left-out feeling, which they find difficult to describe because of the guilt they have about the feeling. They do not feel sorry for themselves. They are mature enough to see this as a hazard of the profession. At the same time they wonder if it needs to be. They do not allow it conscious thought because there seems to be no possibility of change.

In essence, it is a kind of discrimination, most pronounced in the area of their social life. Since pastors have little time for anything but responsibilities relating to the church, the social needs of their wives suffer. Your minister's wife is not devoid of *activity*, but often she feels apart and alone since she is not supposed to express herself socially as do members of the congregation. This revelation will, no doubt, evoke wonderment—surely amazement.

"Why, our minister's wife is very fulfilled socially. She comes to church all the time, teaches our young people every Sunday morning, goes to all the women's meetings, attends mother-and-daughter banquets, and sometimes is invited to religious luncheons. She greets strangers on Sunday and talks to all the members. When our minister is asked to give the invocation for a community banquet, she gets to sit at the head table."

Correct! Except for one word. The social register to which our minister's wife belongs is full. That does not mean she is fulfilled. All are religious, church-related, or community-service functions. (Interestingly, she is not free to visit any church other than her own. She knows what kind of rumors would result.) Her social register says, "Mrs. Minister, this is the world in which you belong. Do not go outside of it."

Some wives may find complete fulfillment and may be comfortable staying within the area of church activities. It may not occur to some to do otherwise, out of habit or tradition, though they should have the right to choose.

Some lay people are beginning to see a need for a change of pace for their clergy couple. They do invite them out for light entertainment or for some athletic event. Many take them out to dinner. This is appreciated, because of their thoughtfulness and because most clergy do not have within their budget provision for eating at nice restaurants. That, probably, is the extent of their social life, unless one includes attendance at the children's school concerts as a social event.

An unwritten law prohibits the pastor's wife and her husband from invitations to banquets, charity balls, and other occasions that include interesting speakers, comedians, and celebrities. She may be asked to speak, present a program on ceramics, or perform for groups and clubs, but she is not invited to participate in them regularly, or to join. Why?

1. *We didn't think to ask her.* If so, it is a grievous oversight.

2. *She is different.* From whom? From what? How? By whose definition? She, too, was a baby, a little girl, a young woman—like everybody else; and unique—like everybody else. Then she married. She immediately became different. Is it because she married a minister?

3. *She is too busy.* If so, maybe the demands upon her and her husband should be lessened. A staff helper should be hired. Lay people who have time for their social expression could lend a hand in the work of the church, so she would have time for hers.

4. *She would not be interested.* Should she not be consulted about that?

5. *She would not fit in.* Who or what determines who fits in? The church—the group to which she and

her husband are giving themselves, helps everyone who comes to fit in. Would some of the people who are thus accepted deny her acceptance into their group?

6. *She does not have the social needs other women do.* Wrong! One hundred percent! She may have more, because she is constantly fragmented by what persons and groups expect—and demand—of her. She needs a time to be put back together. She is at all times on display. She desperately needs to be taken out of the showcase for a few hours, or a few days, to enjoy anonymity and the rarity of being, not different but like, others. Total social diversion from her role would be refreshing and restorative.

7. *She is not qualified.* There may be requirements, common interests and hobbies, educational standards, or status considerations. She may not meet them. Fair enough. However, if she does, and continues to be overlooked, think about this. Your minister's wife begins a special training and education from the day she steps into the ministry. When it comes to adapting, learning, adjusting, developing her gifts, handling varied—often delicate—situations, and relating to all kinds of people, she is distinctly qualified. Indeed she may be one of the most interesting people you will be privileged to know.

A lovely young woman shared the following experience: Her ambition was to be an actress, and she worked hard to achieve her goal. Her life took a dramatic turn when she met, and later married, a young man training for the Christian ministry. Their first little church was in a fashionable suburban community. One of her husband's first weddings was that of a young couple from two socially prominent families. It was to be a formal wedding in grand style —tuxedo, black tie, white gloves for the men and elegant gowns for the ladies. She was invited, of course, and reminded periodically that everyone was to be formally attired.

"We couldn't afford it, but I bought a beautiful, much too expensive dress. I rationalized that in our community I would have many other opportunities to wear it. Couples in our congregation attended many lovely social events. They described them glowingly—the speakers, the celebrities, and the guests they invited to go with them. I was sure we would be invited, sometimes, to be their guests.

"The wedding was four years ago," she said wistfully. "My beautiful gown is fading in the closet. I can't wear it to concerts, because the only seats we can afford are in the top balcony, and I would look ridiculous." Looking down, as though ashamed to tell her deep, dark secret, she added, "Sometimes, when I am sure no one else is in the house, I take out my dress carefully, and, like my little girls playing dress-up, put it on. As I dream and promenade before the mirror I ask myself, or maybe I am asking God, 'Do we have to give up everything but church things because others say so?' I wouldn't trade my life—or my charming-prince preacher —for anybody. But," her choked voice trailed off, "it would be fun, just once, to be Cinderella!"

Does this kind of "frivolity" belong in the life of a woman married to a minister—or in this book? Of course it does. "My God will supply every need of yours according to his riches." (Phil. 4:19 RSV) does not mean bare subsistence necessities. Each person has many needs, and God has limitless riches to supply them. He put them within those whom he created: esthetic, expressive, acceptance, love, social needs.

He was democratic about endowing us with these needs. He did not line up x number of people over here and proclaim, "These are your needs." Then another line over there, "Because you are to be spiritual leaders, shepherds, pastors, ministers—and wives—these are not your needs."

Your pastor's wife's social life is not to be *prescribed* for her like a medical prescription: "Rx—take only church-related activities four times daily." Neither is it to be *proscribed* by withholding from her all social expressions because of the profession of the man she married. Archaic attitudes prevent her from developing intimate friendships in or out of the church. There is a big wide wonderful world of beautiful people and things in addition to the one where she is kept in confinement. Will she be freed to discover them?

Divorce for a pastor and his wife? Heaven forbid! That is not possible. A minister does not get divorced. It's too bad when people do, but not ministers! Have you heard a similar statement or had that feeling? Have you totally rejected it? If your pastor got a divorce, would you reject him? A shocking idea? Then what about this shocking fact:

> The dangerous practice of becoming all things to all people, and conforming to roles which are not real, can all have a devastating effect on marriage. So much so, that *among professionals, clergymen rank third in the number of divorces granted each year.*[2]

The alarming rise of divorce does not exclude clergymen. The best of marriages in average families have difficulties that need constant hard work. But the minister and his family are not average. They must be exemplary—in church, in public, in school, or in the grocery store. If they are not, they will be more noticed than other people. The quotes from the ministers' wives surveyed reveal the resentment many feel as they see their husbands burning themselves out for others, leaving little time for their own families.

The pressures on the minister and his family cannot be turned inward and ignored. They don't go away. Someplace there must be release. Since it cannot be done elsewhere, a pastor's home—his castle—becomes an armed fortress! One partner or the other may blow up at something said, when they both know it was not the remark but the pressure build-up of days, weeks, and months. Though they love each other deeply, they hurt for the hurt of one another. They are in this sorry state because there is never time for them to grow together in what was once their most important com-mitment—their marriage.

I know of several divorced ministers who entered the ministerial profession in the later years of their marriage. When I had a chance to discuss with them the reasons for the divorce, both partners agreed they could not take the pressures, idealistic as was their intent when they entered the ministry. Some are thinking, "How awful! Weren't those people in the ministry dedicated? How could they possibly do this in God's work?"

Yet they know, within their immediate circle, many friends who have gone through divorce. Are the vows taken by a lay couple less binding than those taken by clergy couples? We are speaking primarily about Christians. A conservative estimate would be that at least 5 percent of church members are divorced. That would mean that at least 500,000 people who have experienced divorce claim some form of church membership![3]

During the phone conversation with the man who ministered to me, he reflected concern, bordering on alarm, about deteriorating communication between pastors and their wives. He meets regularly with a group of pastors who share common problems and needs. The discussions of late have gravitated to their marriages. Was it possible to strike a balance between the demands of their careers and a healthy relationship with their wives and families? One man expressed a troubled feeling with which the rest readily identified:

> About the time I think I have found a balance and get everything in order for time with my family, another church crisis rears its head. My resolution not to answer the phone during dinner, to play a game with the kids, or to sit with my wife and listen to her, evaporates, and I tear out of the house. It has become so commonplace that when I announce, with happy satisfaction, that a particular time has been cleared for them, my wife tenses for the inevitable let-down, and the kids give me a "We've heard that before, Dad."

Another pastor was deeply disturbed that while for hours he can empathize with the problems of Helen, Jane, or Laura to the point where he is able to tell them about his feelings, sometimes his marriage, he cannot communicate with his wife. When, eventually, he gets home, emotionally spent, he is too tired to listen to her concerns. This man verbalized what was common to all in the group.

What happens to the wife? She knows he listens to the problems of many women, and she feels threatened because he has no time or energy to listen to her. Since he is overburdened, she conditions herself not to add additional burdens or to engage in light talk. He is all talked out and listened out. As a result, husband and wife push down layer upon layer of feelings, which remain there and petrify. All communication—talking, loving, laughing, inconsequentials—grinds to a hopeless halt. They both know they are losing touch with the only person in the world they love and care about. They are lonely, hurt, empty.

The wife begins to believe the parishers' feelings—that she is different. She convinces herself that she has it all together. She is tough, efficient, self-sufficient, and does not have the needs other women do. She can't allow herself to have problems, with her husband having to attend to those of others. The kids are doing quite well, though most of the time she has to be mother and father. They are all generally well liked by the congregation. What more could she want? Thus, in addition to society's image, she adds her own manufactured image of the minister's wife. And of one thing she becomes increasingly aware. To be married to a minister means to give him away.

Two pastors met for lunch. They talked shop for several hours, and tried to impress one another with how conscientiously they pursued their pastoring. Neither ever took a day off. To prove their point they pulled out their date books. One of the men proudly declared that he was out, away from home, forty-two consecutive nights, in calls and meetings. He settled back to enjoy his victory. It was short-lived. His friend counted forty-four.

Some years later they met and reviewed the incident. The sheer, utter stupidity of their earlier values hit them with full force. They were relieved and grateful that they had both matured enough to recognize that kind of pride.

It is high time pastors and lay people learn what constitutes sane, sensible pastoring. By habitually deferring to the needs or nonneeds of others, and neglecting those who love them the most, pastors pay a terrible price.

Many clergy husbands and wives who seem to have a good relationship may be resolutely functioning in independence and loneliness. Others, who are tired of playing second fiddle and believe there is something more, look in the yellow pages for a lawyer.

Churches are beginning to recognize that divorce happens to ministers too. They recognize that their pastors are over-pressured, and too much is asked of them. For some clergy, divorce means the end of their pastoral career. There is some optimism in that regard. A few churches will keep, or will call, a pastor who has gone through divorce. This is encouraging, but these are still a negligible few.

A discussion such as this must include other members of the family—the minister's children. Clergy parents sensibly have realized for a long time that they must bring them up as normally as possible. They do not expect them to be good examples because "Dad's a minister." They teach them to be examples because of their love for Christ.

It is tempting for a congregation to idolize pastors' children when they are little and cute. But as they grow up and do the things other children do, they are singled out. They seem to be louder, run more, or whatever, when they are just being regular kids. It is important that if they cannot see too much of their father, they should have their mother during the difficult rearing years. Clergy parents have sometimes discovered too late that their children needed them far more than any committees or women's luncheons.

Some pastors' children have been turned off completely, many never to return to a faith they once had, as they witness the time they *don't* have with their parents. Often they are thoroughly disillusioned by the insensitivity and critical spirit of people in their parish, especially as it relates to their parents. They know instinctively those they can trust and those who like or don't like their parents.

If any of you causes one of these little ones who

trusts in me to lose his faith, it would be better for
you to have a rock tied to your neck and be thrown
into the sea. (Matthew 18:6 LB)

God has a higher purpose than any stereotyped image for
the women who are married to ministers—and for their
families. They do not have to do and be certain things
because *others* say so. *God* wants them—like everyone—to
discover who they are and what they are to be. This is our
common heritage in Christ.

Checklist

_____ Examine your attitudes about your pastor's wife. If
they are bad, one small act of kindness will open you
up to each other. If they are good make them better.
If someone had the same attitudes towards you,
would it make you glad or sad?

_____ She needs special friends, too. Someone with whom
she can be herself, who can share her faults and fears.

_____ Help her break out of the mold—the minister's wife
image. Some of the insights in this chapter may help.

_____ Let her know you don't expect her to be "typical."
You could step in when the "image" demands come
along, and help divert them.

_____ Unless she wants to be called "our pastor's wife,"
avoid that description so she will not be on the spot
and make others uncomfortable.

_____ Take her to lunch. Share your common love and
faith. Resist the temptation to shop talk or to give her
a list of oughts for her husband.

_____ Alert yourself and your friends to be on guard when
you and the church *prescribe* and *proscribe* the social

life of your clergy couple. What they should do and where they should go. If it's right for you, it's right for them and conversely.

_____ A kind consideration when calling your pastor's home and his wife answers, is to refrain from starting with "Since I can't get hold of your husband, who is too busy, I'll tell you. . . ." She does not want to be rude by refusing to listen; there is nothing she can do about the problem anyway; and she takes upon herself *his* mountain-of-things-I-didn't-get-done guilt, making her less effective when he needs her to help him forget the cares of the day.

_____ Be normal to the minister's normal children. *Never* find fault with their parents. If you must, please, never within their hearing.

_____ Invite this woman, married to your pastor, to a group or club, not to be on the program, but to be one of you.

_____ Maybe your minister and his wife are unable to say no to anything asked of them. Help others not to take advantage of this. Help them to say no. Your reward will be a more effective pastor, and you may save a marriage.

_____ Separate her from the profession of her husband. Free her to be a woman! Allow her to be the person God intended her to be.

8

Questions about
HIS PREACHING

For Christ didn't send me to baptize, but to preach
the Gospel. . . . I know very well how foolish it
sounds to those who are lost when they hear that
Jesus died to save them. But we who are saved
recognize this message as the very power of
God. . . . For God in his wisdom saw to it that the
world should never find God through human
brilliance, and then he stepped in and saved all
those who believed his message, which the world
calls foolish and silly. . . . It seems foolish to the
Gentiles because they believe only what agrees with
their philosophy. (1 Cor. 17, 18, 21, 22 LB)

Preaching the good news that God so loved the world that
he gave his Son that we might live abundantly, hope en-
duringly, and die resurrectedly, is the church's primary
purpose and message. Therefore, it is the preacher-pastor's
primary responsibility. It is this "foolishness" that has
withstood distortion by a few preachers and the indifferent
faithlessness on the part of many who call themselves
followers of Christ—the meaning of the word "Christian."

Preaching is the backbone of perpetuating the Christian faith.

We are not sure exactly how the first Christians conducted their worship. Undoubtedly, the influence of synagogue forms was evident. We do know that these devout believers sang, prayed, shared, and studied the Torah—the Old Testament—since the New Testament was not yet in existence. We also know that Paul's letters, or Epistles, were circulated among these young churches, and that he instructed the Christians to read them as they met together. We know, too, that these early Christians were eager for the fellowship of believers in an extremely hostile world. They wanted to know as much as they could about this man called Jesus, who had changed their lives and whose teachings they did not fully understand.

Times are different now, some two thousand years later. Forms of ministry and forms of worship have undergone continuing adaptations. Gone are the days when the preacher's job was to preach once on Sunday mornings in one church and perhaps drive twenty miles to the next town to preach the same sermon Sunday night in rural America. His other tasks were to visit the sick, conduct funerals, and enjoy leisurely home-cooked meals in the homes of his parish. He could visit every home in a short period of time because congregations were small and life simple. If he preached a good sermon and called on the sick he was fulfilling his main obligations to his church.

Contrast that with today's "ministerial haberdashery," the hats he has to wear, the masks he must put on in the roles he has to fulfill—expertly! For years we have been misinterpreting an important truth in the Book of Ephesians:

> Some of us have been given special ability as apostles, to others he has given the gift of being able

> to preach well; some have special ability in winning
> people to Christ, helping them to trust him as their
> Savior; still others have a gift for caring for God's
> people as a shepherd does his sheep, leading and
> teaching them in the ways of God. (Eph. 4:11 LB)

How has that been misinterpreted? Substitute the words
our "minister," or our "pastor," or our "preacher," for the
words "some" and "others." Any one of these abilities should
be sufficient to qualify a pastor as a "man sent by God." Add
to these just a few of the roles or "hats" discussed in other
chapters. That is just a subtotal. How about patience,
discipline, spirituality, kindness, diplomacy, a noncritical
spirit (have you ever heard your pastor criticize or gossip
about one person to another?), love, goodness, generosity,
and all other expected virtues. In our complex days,
preaching is but the tip of the pastor's iceberg. It should be
his foremost responsibility, and he has so little time to do
justice to it—both in preparing the message and preparing
himself to preach it.

Nowhere in Scripture does one find that all preachers must
be eloquent, profound orators, possess excellent vocal
timbre, be handsome, short or tall, and be able to please all
of the people in every message they preach. These "requirements" are of highly recent origin. They came into ascen-
dancy long after the fiery, outspoken, zealous telling-it-like-
it-is preaching of Paul, Peter, Barnabas, Stephen and
Timothy. True, Paul used praise before he punched. But
punch he did! He minced no words in pointing out their
specific sins. Can you imagine how many times a preacher
would dare do that now?

There are thousands of clergymen today who have a whole
bundle of natural abilities, spiritual gifts, and many bonus
qualities, which they apply in their own unique way. Most of
them are good communicators, good preachers, or they

would not be in the ministry. Most, the large majority, have had, in addition, rigorous training and high educational standards, laid down by select boards and educators. (There are the few exceptions—self-appointed, self-styled "preachers"—who are not properly prepared, but who gather a following. They are a small minority, and any thinking person will not be led astray by them.)

When a church sets out to seek a new minister it has many expectations: Is he nice? Is he outgoing? Cordial? Friendly? Does he make a good appearance in the pulpit? Is he "spiritual"? Will he satisfy the parishioner's needs and those of his family? Will he work well with a staff? (It is a great disservice and breach of etiquette to insist that a new pastor keep the staff members of a previous administration. He may or may not want to, after careful consideration, but that choice should be his, backed up clearly and explicitly by all boards and committees.) Can he administrate? Can he get us out of debt? Will he appeal to young people? Is he too intellectual for some, or is he intellectual enough for young college people? How much do we have to pay him?

Someplace at the bottom of this interminable list one might find the question, "Does he preach well?"—meaning to many: "Is his pulpit manner and the way he speaks going to please me?" That should not be the question. The question that should be asked is, "Does he bear faithful witness to God's love for everyone?"

A church may feel it has the greatest preacher available, and before long it is taking that ability, the most important part of his ministry, for granted. Church laity may then begin to place their emphasis on all the other things they expect of him. A few have short memories about all of his career's attendant responsibilities when he faithfully carries them out and zero in on some small thing that he may not have had time to do.

How may worshippers prepare for the pastor's preaching?

It is not accidental that I use the word "worshippers" instead of "audience." I prefer the use of the word "sanctuary" to "auditorium" as related to a religious experience. An "audience" listens. An "auditorium" is a place in which one listens. "Worshipping" involves participation.

A "sanctuary" is a sacred place of refuge—a place set apart to meet God. It can be in your home, in your car, or in a church building. But it is a place where there is interaction between you and God. Your worship in your sanctuary prepares you to receive the sermon.

Another way for the person in the pew to be prepared for and blessed through worship with others is *to be there.* Absenteeism among church members, Christians, believers is shameful! Attendance on any given Sunday includes well under half the total recorded church membership of our country. Catholics are the highest attenders, Protestants next, and Jewish members the lowest. Two-thirds of all Protestant members attend rarely, if at all.

Out of this two-thirds, interestingly enough, come some of the loudest rumblings. If they catch a rumor flying about something happening in (all of a sudden) "my" church, they quickly show interest, especially if it is something with which they do not agree. They are usually not interested enough to get the facts. It's easier to store bits of misinformation and accumulate prejudices. One faithful member, after listening for years to a grumbling nonattender, heard one complaint too many. She remarked, "If you want to find out what's wrong with the church, just ask somebody who doesn't go!"

Many nonattending church members use the well-worn excuse, "I can worship God anyplace. I don't have to go to church." Right! On both counts! You can and should worship at all times and everywhere—but *do you?* You don't have to go to church to commune with God. No one can make you go to church. But your pastor and spiritually growing Christian friends know the value of getting together with other Christians and listening to God through music, through prayer, and through the message from the pulpit. If you are not going, you probably are not growing. Ask someone who uses this excuse for not going to worship when they last really, truly, deeply, and seriously worshipped and listened for God's voice in their lives. You will receive a graduate course in the art of evasion.

What do these people—who, at some time, confessed to accepting Christ as Lord—do with these instructions from the writer of Hebrews:

> In response to all He has done for us, let us out-do each other in being helpful and kind to each other and doing good. Let us not neglect our church meetings, as some people do, but encourage and warn each other, especially now that the day of his coming back again is drawing near. (Heb. 10:24, 25 LB)

(In saying all of this, there is, of course, consideration for the ill and the incapacitated, who cannot go to a church building to worship. Perhaps they are the true worshippers, whose entire dependence is upon God. Many include in their worship a prayer for their pastor and his church.)

Not only is your purpose for being in a church assembly worship, praying, and sharing, it is also an act of obedience. God set the first example on the seventh day when he himself rested from his work. He demanded regular and definite times of worship for his people. Jesus regularly attended the synagogue on the Sabbath. (Luke 4:16 AV) Meeting together strengthens the whole body of Christian believers and brings renewal to every member of that body. "Misery loves company." How much more, though, does "happiness."

THEY CRY, TOO!

There is something unusual about the person who does not want to share a happiness. There must be others to share it with. A bundle of sticks makes a nice warm fire. One stick taken out of the fire and put off by itself goes out. Christians taken out of the fellowship of purifying fire "go out," too.

The pastor, too, must prepare for worship. Studying and creating his message week after ceaseless week is difficult and draining. More than that, he must be prepared for the needs of his worshippers. He must keep in mind constantly their life situations: A couple is heading toward divorce; a mother is dying of cancer; an employer is worried about his business; a teenage girl is pregnant; someone is upset with the pastor; someone has a problem with alcohol; two members sitting across the aisle aren't speaking; a wife sitting alone in her church prays for her husband. There are as many needs as there are people. This man sent by God must speak to each of those needs.

As he rises to give God's message of love and grace to this sea of faces, the pastor realizes once again that he has been called to an impossible task. He knows, too, that a strange and wonderful something happens as God's Spirit takes mere words and transforms them into living reality—if the worshipper is prepared.

But the Adversary is on twenty-four-hour duty to prevent this from happening. The roadblocks he puts up are extremely varied and clever. He takes normal situations and high ideals and twists them in remarkable ways to achieve his ends. Some of his most diabolical schemes are at work, not during the week but on the Sabbath, or Sunday morning.

One of his favorite tricks is to get the worshipper's mind off the truths presented, and onto other things: It may be a family fight before church; whether the oven was turned on to cook the dinner; or who will win Sunday's ball game. These are obvious, and people with any spiritual sensitivity quickly become aware of them. It is the distortions of worship that are invidious.

The person in the pew wants and needs something worthwhile from the pulpit. No one desires that more than the preacher, though it is a frightening, never-ending assignment. He may not be able to hit a home run every Sunday of the year. A spiritually tuned-in worshipper understands and derives joy from every part of the service. But Satan is wily, and he persists. He has won many a battle over a good-turned-evil. Sometimes he wins people for a time by using a simple phrase to raise havoc. A good example of this is the phrase "good preaching." This means something different to each one present, since everyone is different.

To some, good preaching means hearing the same terminology in every sermon—or the gospel, the truth, the word has not been preached. Clichés, to these people, are their theological security blanket, so tightly knit around them that they are incapable of stretching a centimeter. Part of this stems from a rigid background. Ignorance of the higher Biblical truths, rather than wooden legalistic literalism, is another influence.

To others, good preaching means that which contains Scripture read out of the King James Version. As in the case of the little lady who refused any translation but that one.

"Because," she pronounced, "that is the language my Lord spoke." One may chuckle at this, but it illustrates some of the nit-picking people engage in.

Oratory that tickles the ears and appeals to the ego or intellect is the definition of still others. One likes conversational preaching, while another still equates good preaching with pulpit-pounding and sizable sonority. Some want their preacher to be authentic and real, while others do not want his humanity to show.

In themselves, these varying ideas about good preaching

are neither right nor wrong. When they are allowed to be the only measuring rod and are forced on others, then they become a good turned evil.

Another one of the tempter's tricks is using people as passive pawns in the worship meeting. He knows that religion is boring for those who watch! Smiling, laughing, shaking hands, embracing a friend, clapping for joy, singing out joyfully—these are "no-no's" to him. Better that his captives of the hour be preoccupied, angry, tense, or sleepy. These are acceptable behaviors to Satan. His counsel is: "Do go to worship, but don't get involved."

The Adversary also likes to discredit the minister through seemingly innocent remarks about his preaching. They become a preacher's pet peeves:

> Why don't you ever preach about . . . ? [He did, you weren't there.]
>
> Your sermons are too deep for me.
>
> Your preaching should have more Bible and less illustrations.
>
> Why don't you use more stories in your sermons?
>
> Why don't you preach against . . . [meaning things I don't do].
>
> Your sermons are too long.
>
> I only come to hear your sermons, pastor. Why don't you preach longer?
>
> I don't like the present series you are preaching

about. [They only believe what agrees with their philosophy.] (1 Cor. 1:22 LB)

Unless you are in the pulpit, pastor, I don't feel like I've been to church.

A pastor is not flattered by people who stay away if he is not in the pulpit. Rather, it causes him to wonder if his ministry will ever help you see that your first commitment is to Christ—and that includes his church.

This does not begin to describe Satan's bundle of nefarious schemes to keep people from worshipping, though they may be in church physically. But he saves his most despicable plan, that will work when all others fail. This devious dynamic affects virtually millions of church members with inordinate regularity. I call it Satan's Sunday Cel-Abrasion!

When I was a child, getting our family of seven ready for church was a major misadventure. This was before automatic washing machines, dishwashers, cartoned milk and eggs (these came from original sources), permapress fabrics, and hair dryers. Before showers, too, since there was no central running water system in our little village. Much preparation was done on Saturday—weekly baths, hair washed and rolled in rag strips, Sunday dresses, pants, and shirts carefully washed and pressed by hand. Sunday school lessons were read and studied, under Dad's watchful eye, around the family table.

Nevertheless, Sunday morning always managed to get out of hand. We kids hollered at each other, Mother and Dad hollered back and became upset with each other. I suspect all the other families in our little church shared the same Sunday Cel-Abrasion, as we stood together, ashamed and guilty, mumbling, "This is the day which the Lord hath made. Let us rejoice and be glad in it." (Ps. 118:24 AV)

THEY CRY, TOO!

As I look back, I realize that we need not have felt that badly about it. Here were seven people getting in each other's way trying to meet the same deadline. This, without conveniences, in a very small space and in a very short time, regardless of how early we got up. I think we did amazingly well. However, my guilt feelings reached such proportions I vowed it would never happen in my home. You guessed it. It did! Sometimes still does! With each additional future church member born into our private congregation, the Sunday pandemonium increases.

My husband left home earlier every Sunday to avoid the chaos and prepare himself for his preaching responsibility. He couldn't seem to find the inspiration he needed with someone yelling, "When can I get into the bathroom?" Despite all my gadgets, with no cows to milk, fixing breakfast and getting dressed became a hassle that surpassed that of my childhood. Always, at the last minute, I would grab kids, lipstick, diaper bag, and stuff these items into the car.

After depositing my arguing, crying, perpetual-motion aggregate in Sunday School and nursery, I would paste a smile over my scowl to greet friends and strangers. I would enter the sanctuary to worship Almighty God. There I was again—the child—guilty and ashamed, as I stood with the congregation, mumbling, "This is the day . . ." Satan was still at it, having his Sunday Cel-Abrasion. I prayed for forgiveness.

As we have become less afraid of being honest, many many people have admitted that they, too, experience the same scene, as do the other families they know. I have no qualms in suggesting that there are Sunday tensions in 99 percent of all Christian homes. Each of these probably believes, as we did, that their family is the only one to whom this happens. And it is not limited to families with children. It happens to couples, both young and old. One of these beautiful couples admitted: "Satan starts early in our home. We have our biggest fights on Saturday night. Why does it happen when we are studying to teach our Sunday morning class? It's a cinch we don't want it that way. It has to be a force outside ourselves."

That is Satan's Sunday Cel-Abrasion fifty-two times a year—noisy bedlam or covert hostility. He has manipulated ordinary family confusion into crises and wounding abrasions. Though these millions of families are at church, it doesn't bother him a bit. With his prepreaching, preteaching upheaval, how could anyone be prepared to meet God? How could guilt, embarrassment, and alienation open up minds and hearts to the message the messenger has painstakingly prepared? How gleeful Satan must be!

What can be done to turn this around? First, it should be put into proper and practical perspective. Despite labor-saving devices, easy-care clothing and multiple bathrooms, life is infinitely complex. Everyone in the family has differing and varied interests occupying the mind. During the week, members of the family get ready for school or work at different hours. On the Sabbath or Sunday, everybody has the same deadline. Enter confusion, normal abrasive action and reaction, and a pile-up in the bathroom. All right, it happens! Expect it! Accept and know he understands. If this is done, Satan is not winning!

When impatience and anger linger and follow us out the door, to the car, and into our teaching or worship sanctuary, it ceases to be normal family confusion and becomes sinful and destructive. That is Satan's Sunday Cel-Abrasion winning! Think what would happen if millions of families struck back at him! Expecting, accepting, forgetting, and thanking our Lord for a temptation put down, would deal a devastating blow to the enemy. This massive strike-back would become a monumental setback! Satan's Sunday Cel-Abrasion would be turned around to become God's victorious celebration!

You will be prepared for worship. You will not only get the message—you will want to give it! You will be like those in the parable of the sower who "listen to God's words and cling to them and steadily spread them to others who also soon believe." (Luke 8:15 LB)

Your pastor, that person this book is all about, who has given a large part of his life to prepare something worthwhile for you, will be thrilled by your responsiveness.

And through the foolishness of preaching, a miracle will happen to a prepared people. A strange, wondrous encounter with God himself. As he reaches down, his creation reaches up, and they touch in each other, the Divine Nature.

Checklist

_____ To get the most out of your pastor's preaching, you must be there physically and prepared mentally and spiritually.

_____ With your family, develop good mental hygiene about getting ready physically and preparing spiritually long before your worship day. Think about meeting God on Sunday, not stuffing church—one more activity—into your weekend.

_____ As God instructed his people in the Old Testament, do everything that needs to be done the day before worship, so you can concentrate on true worship.

_____ As a family-togetherness project you might discuss how to prepare for worship. Specific duties could be assigned each member of the family.

_____ Part of your family-worship training program should

include respect for being on time for teaching and worship hours.

_____ Avoid preachers' pet peeves.

_____ Now that you may have gained insight into who tries to destroy your worship, try to cut family confusion to a minimum. If you fail—and you will—Satan cannot usurp the opportunity for evil unless you let him. Remember, expect it, accept it, most important, *forget it!*

_____ Go into your worship with happy intentions. Leave your "sacred cows" outside and open up to new ways and ideas. You will enjoy the table God has prepared for you, as you listen to his message through his messenger—custom-made just for you!

9
Questions about
HIS CHURCH

... as Christ loved the church ... (Eph. 5:25)

There is a term that has been bandied about generously for some years. It refers to a group or to groups of people not in the mainstream of society—minority groups who don't fit into traditional molds and have different, sometimes strange, life-styles. The term is subculture. These subcultures are not readily accepted by society and are fighting for their rights, many with success. Though they may not be popular, some have produced considerable shock waves.

It is not without caution but with increasing conviction that I suggest that a large, long-established traditional segment of society is included in this category by default. This group is the clergy, whom millions of people still regard as different. *The Yearbook of American and Canadian Churches*, reports a total of 250 religious bodies, over 300,000 churches, 131 million inclusive members and 400,000 clergy—a sizable minority. *One of the last minorities to be freed!*

Sadly these men and women, sent or called by God to serve, are often made to feel they do not belong to the mainstream of society. A generation or two ago, their roles were clearly defined. But they, too, have felt the impact of change as much or more than other groups, since they deal with all social types. To most lay people they still appear to be a bit odd, and don't function quite as "normal" people do.

They eat lots of fried chicken, and give invocations at public gatherings in smoke-filled halls. They get up behind pulpits on Sunday mornings to do their thing and relax, sleep, and play golf the other six days of the week.

Mr. John C. Harris, Director of Clergy Training of the Episcopal Dioceses of Maryland and Washington, writes:

> The necessary consensus among Christians about the purpose of the local church has collapsed, and there has been an accompanying loss of agreement about the role of the minister. . . . Predictably a loss of consensus about purpose carries with it a crisis of leadership. As minister during the past decade, we have seen a steady drift of ministers out of the church. . . . Edgar W. Mills and John P. Koval, who studied stress patterns in the ministries of nearly 5,000 Protestant clergy, found that almost two-thirds of the ministers reported the largest source of occupational stress in their relationships with parishioners. Thirty percent of these ministers specified growing stress out of personal or ideological conflict with members. Even more striking perhaps, Mills and Koval found that one-fifth of the responding ministers felt their work in the church to be futile or ineffectual, with one minister in eight finding a stress area "sufficiently serious to cause him to consider secular employment."[1]

There is a great need for people to love their church as

Christ loves it. The reference to "his" church in the chapter title needs to be clarified. We all know it is God's—*his* Church—the universal body of believers. A particular church is part of that larger Church. Some people object to their pastor calling the church they serve *my* church. If these folks would realize what he means they would be flattered. Rarely does a pastor speak with other than pride about his church.

One of the questions in the clerical survey referred to in chapter 1 was "What are the most encouraging and rewarding areas of the clergy's work?" These were some of the answers as leaders spoke for their pastors:

> Seeing people grow spiritually
> Working with young people
> Evangelism and hospital ministry
> Counseling
> Celebrating the Eucharist
> Helping establish new Christian homes
> A sense of helping others and leading in the worship of God
> Fellowship of other Christians
> Being a minister to ministers
> Helping bring about reconciliation
> People coming into a right relationship with Christ
> Growing with people
> Feeling the love of parishioners towards the pastor
> Seeing love in the congregation
> Long-time church memberships being renewed
> Ministering to people in crises

These are some of the things that make a pastor love his church. If he, a man, can feel this kind of love, it expresses in miniature the way God must love his church, all his people, including those who displease him.

In the same survey, these were some of the responses to the question, "What are some of the things that discourage clergy the most?"

Declining caliber of leadership, with little appreciation of clergy goals
Unresponsiveness
Inflexible lay persons
Lethargy and apathy of members
Effects of culture shock
Inadequate salaries
Smallness of people
Unconcern for things of the church
Those who would actually undermine the program of the church
Ingrowth
Lack of communication between church officers and pastors
Lack of facilities
Misunderstanding of pastors' positions
Little appreciation
Overcriticism
Indifference toward spiritual things
Congregational disunity
Unwillingness to become involved
Pettiness and demands of parishioners
Bickering
An unsympathetic press
Factionalism
Ingratitude
Trying to make the church suit someone's own selfish and idiotic notions
Lack of clarity in role of minister

The comments speak for themselves. However, one senses

that only the top layer of feeling has emerged and that beneath is buried much more. To the question, "Do you feel the relationship between pastor and laity could be improved?" an overwhelming 100 percent answered "Yes!" including the exclamation mark! To the question, "How?" the response that summed it up the best was "greater understanding of role expectancy on each part. Yet, both clergy and laity prefer avoidance and withdrawal to confrontation and conciliation."

It would be unfair to suggest that other occupations and professions do not have their share of stress. But they have been explored and discussed at length before the public. They have spokesmen to help solve some of their problems. There are associations for doctors and lawyers, lobbyists for nearly any group, unions for trades people. There are riots, sit-ins, stand-ins, lie-ins, strikes, demonstrations, and civil disobedience for other minorities.

Although there have been a few isolated voices crying in the wilderness for consideration of some of the problems of the clergy, little or no attention has been given to those responsible for the spiritual life of our country.

The office of the presidency is considered the most high-pressure job in the world. There is no question that whoever holds that position has tremendous burdens. But complex and thorough measures are taken to protect and take pressures off the president, so he can run the affairs of state. He is guarded against unnecessary and undue strain in daily routine.

> The White House, when used correctly, can be a veritable fortress, not against the great burdens of office, but against the daily irritants and frustrations which can enervate a person as much as anything. . . . [the president] can dwell in the protective layer he chooses, moving from total

loneliness to the degree of exposure he wants for any particular moment. . . .

This private world is pretty complete. It contains a swimming pool, gymnasium, helicopter pad, flower arranger, art collection, grape arbor, masseur, physician, barbershop, theater, herb garden, library, putting green, children's playground, bomb shelter, flower garden, dog kennel, tennis court, and all other facilities for living and working. . . . What isn't there can be summoned from the outside.[2]

In addition, there are valets, servants, secretaries, accountants, speechwriters, chauffeurs, planes, and several homes to which he can retreat. As the office has grown, the need for convenience, privacy, and relief from enervating details, has become imperative.

Leaders in government, national, state, and local; professional people; corporation executives; and union leaders have available to them many such accommodations.

Clergymen—who have all the pressures of leadership, planning, administration, writing, speaking, counseling, comforting, and diplomacy—are almost totally lacking in any of these services. They limp along with little help and never enough time. In addition, they have to be concerned about an old car needing repair, a leaking roof, mowing the lawn, painting the house, preparing income tax returns, and the drudgery of deciding which church or personal bills should be paid out of a too-small income.

These stress factors are, in themselves, enough to boggle the mind, yet thoughtless church members add many more! Etiquette involves understanding, courtesy, and kindness. It also involves manners. In the church, where these virtues should find their highest expression, they are often completely lacking. When we visit other people's homes, we observe certain amenities. We respect that home as belonging to someone else and are careful not to let our children run wild or to open the closet or refrigerator. We don't put our feet up on the couch with shoes on.

When we go to a concert, we don't talk, write notes, poke people, and giggle. If we or our youngsters should do that, someone would promptly condemn such irresponsible behavior. We act appropriately at weddings, funerals, lines at the supermarket, and wait respectfully in doctors' offices. In the church—our sanctuary and God's house—it seems that anything goes. People talk loudly during the prelude, which should be a time of preparation to meet God. Young people and adults poke each other, whisper, write notes, and show their indifference or boredom. Children run in the halls, while parents expect the church staff to discipline them. (If they do, the pastor will hear about it in short order.) Our church manners during worship and other meetings could be vastly improved.

Far more disturbing, however, are the manners of members who make it their business to complicate the work of the church. They have made the proper confession of faith in Christ, have been baptized, and claim the privileges and rights of membership. With most, this is a deep commitment. They realize that the church is the only institution that will allow anyone to attend and that requires only one qualification for membership: faith! Many church members would not qualify for membership in any other group or club. A beautiful commentary about Christ's Church! The most unlovely are welcomed and received—critics to the contrary. Pastors and members bend over backwards to receive them warmly into their fellowship.

With others, commitment is just a word. They are guilty of doing many of the rude things mentioned above. They have no church etiquette—or little of any kind. Just as a congregation observes the qualities, strengths, weaknesses, and conduct of its pastor, so he, too, can spot these kinds of people in his congregation. Though they may think it doesn't show, they are deluding themselves.

Let's put a magnifying glass on some of them and their church etiquette—or lack of it—as seen by the minister.

There is a small nucleus in every church community who are nomads! They are recycled Christians who travel from church to church, looking for the perfect church. Of course, it has to fit their description! They are like the nomad wanderers of the desert who see a mirage. Ah-ha! At last! They have found the perfect church! A few weeks or months later, they're wandering about in the desert again. Maybe their perfect church means a certain kind of music—country, highbrow, lowbrow, whatever. Maybe their perfect church insists the pastor be Johnny-on-the-spot at all times. It might mean hearing in a certain way exactly what they want to hear, phrases that must be in every sermon—or it doesn't contain the whole truth. They confuse absolute sameness in belief with oneness in Christ. When they leave, they leave with the same attitude with which they came, "I didn't expect to find it there, anyway."

The tragedy is what it does when children are involved. At a Sunday school convention a teacher asked how one copes with the child of a nomad family. She had a youngster in her class who would be gone periodically for several weeks, then appear again. After observing this pattern for some months, and after encouraging him to attend regularly, one day she asked him where he was on the missing Sundays. "Oh," he replied with bravado, "my dad's lookin' for a decent church. He doesn't like this one, but it's better than some of the others we've been visiting." He giggled—the class giggled. Every time he came after that disclosure, it was impossible to get the class to listen to, or accept, anything the teacher had prepared. As these Sunday school workers discussed the problem, they could, with some accuracy, predict what would happen to that child. Many had seen it happen before. He would grow up with a cynical view of churches, teachers, and pastors. He would not take seriously any of the Bible that was being taught. As soon as he was old enough, he would refuse to go to Sunday school. Eventually, he would reject the church totally. He would fall back on saying "that church is not good enough!" What an awful responsibility rests on that father, who can't find a church to suit him.

> For there is going to come a time when people won't listen to the truth but will go around looking for teachers who will tell them just what they want to hear. They won't listen to what the Bible says but will blithely follow their own misguided ideas. (2 Tim. 4:3, 4 LB)

One woman summed it up well when she told some no-mads, "One of these days you're going to run out of churches!"

Then there are the "yes-mads." These are members who are in the looking-for-something-to-be-mad-about business. Once they find it, they pounce on it gleefully, "I knew I'd find something to be mad about!" They like to feel that the church is out to get them. If they would be contented just to be mad, that would be great. But they want to make everyone as mad and miserable as they are. They know they are wrong, but they want approval for their attitudes and conduct. So they work on other Christians, stirring the pot, trying to cause discontent about something people wouldn't ordinarily give a second thought.

One thing about the "yes-mads" is that you can always depend on them. They will always be mad about everything!

Another thing you can depend on is that good people get the message and steer clear of them. The extra-special Christians will pray for them and for the pastor to demonstrate an extra measure of love for these who put additional stress on him. Legitimate pressure challenges him. Pettiness debilitates!

> You were getting along so well. Who has interfered with you to hold you back from following the truth? It certainly isn't God who has done it, for He is the one who has called you to freedom in Christ. But it takes only one wrong person among you to infect all the others. . . . God will deal with that person, whoever he is, who has been troubling and confusing you. (Gal. 5:7–10 LB)

Then there are church *takers.* They take everything the church can give to them free. Baby-sitting for their children on Sunday mornings, while they sleep or watch the ball game. They call the pastor to pray for the sick relative, or ask him to straighten out their kids or their marriage. Mostly they don't bother to go to church. They may want their children to participate in the youth activities, but they give nothing of themselves or their money to help their own youngsters.

Some of the most annoying members are the "you-oughters"! These "otters" are as busy as beavers trying to figure out ways to keep the pastor, his wife, and his kids busy with things "you-oughter" do, just because you are the pastor, or his wife, or his kids.

Another category are church *users.* They use the church for a picturesque wedding and don't come back again until it is time to show off the baby at a dedication, or a baptism ceremony. Others use the church to make a good image in the community, or for career betterment. Then, too, belonging to a church will look good in the obituary column some day.

There is the true story of a man who boasted that, although he was a member, he had not set foot inside of his church for thirty years. When a business meeting was called to decide whether or not the present church property should be sold in order to purchase a larger location for the growing church, he decided it was about time to go. He ostentatiously marched down to the front pew for the important meeting. The pastor, who had been in the church eight years, didn't know who he was, though he had attempted to call on the man. When it was time to vote, the thirty-year dropout shouted a resounding "no!" and walked out, to wait another thirty years.

Some church users are not so obvious. A midwest pastor told about an attractive couple who began attending his church. After a few weeks they asked for an appointment to see him, which he granted. They had both been divorced from previous marriages. For that reason their own church would not marry them. They asked this pastor if he would consent to marry them. They gave every impression that they intended to make this their church home. They indicated that they would rededicate themselves to be worthy of being married with the blessing and approval of the church.

The ever-increasing problem of divorce poses a serious and painful dilemma for the clergyman. To stand firmly on the principle of "no exception," i.e., that he will not marry them, or give the sanction of his sacred office, in the hope that he will be instrumental in keeping them in contact with the church, is weighed each time he is confronted with this situation.

The pastor told the couple he would think about it. They attended church faithfully and seemed to be maturing, responsible Christians. After a few months the pastor consented to marry them. Attendance at first was regular, then it became sporadic. They gave up the responsibilities they had asked for in the church. They gradually dropped out and disappeared. Later it was learned that they had gone back to their former church, after going through the motions of using another church to accomplish their ends, the sanction of a church wedding. In order to explain this to friends, they evidently encountered some "yes-mads" along the way, and began to point out all the things that were wrong in the church they had used. In this way, they tried to justify their actions.

> Each of us is a part of the one body of Christ. . . . If one part suffers, all parts suffer with it, and if one part is honored, all the parts are glad. (1 Cor. 12:13, 26 LB)

Another kind of church member is the spiritual thrill seeker. These people are like an ivy plant with shallow roots and spreading runners, which go in all directions. They, too, run in all directions after this spiritual experience, that ecstasy, or some new, superthrilling excitement. They are tasters of whatever latest religious fad hits the community, and have difficulty holding on until the next religious thrill comes along. They never stay with any one thing long enough to put roots down into the richness of God's nurturing soil. They become so conditioned, after nondirectional running hither and yon, that if they do not feel a thrill, ecstasy, or warmth in quiet worship, they are sure that church doesn't have real religion, and they start running again.

They are living a kind of Christian existentialism that puts stress on what they feel rather than who they are. Feeling and existing in the here and now are more important than becoming spiritually mature. Their energies become diffused, and there is none left for depth growing within the Body. They miss the greatest thrill of all, and they do not have to go seeking after it. It is at all times within their grasp. "Be still and know that I am God." (Ps. 46:10)

Nurture that seed within you. Jesus said, "The kingdom of God never comes by watching for it. Men cannot say, 'Look, here it is,' or 'There it is,' for the kingdom of God is inside you." (Luke 17:21 PT) "That seed wants to grow up into a sturdy branch of the true Vine, which cannot, like the clinging vine, be plucked out of His hand." (John 10:28 AV)

There are others too! church-blamers, complainers, ignorers, debunkers, why-do-they-ers, why-don't-they-ers, criticizers, or any combination of these.

It's a good thing most pastors have a good sense of humor. If they don't they'd better acquire one.

The tragedy of this is that, though these people may not care about their attitudes and behavior, though the pastor may understand their attitudes and behavior, though the beautiful are praying about their attitudes and behavior, the world is watching them.

The mission of the church is not to answer, to the point of satiety, the call, "Feed *me*, stuff *me*, entertain *me*, help *me*." The demand of all who say they love Christ should be, "I must minister! Not gorge my ego by devouring negatives. I must feed others with positives! For I am part of the most loving, caring fellowship on earth!"

> Our Father which art in heaven,
> Hallowed be thy name.
> Thy kingdom come,
> Thy will be done. . . .
> Through this imperfect me
> Through my imperfect church
> in this imperfect world
> to make it more like heaven.

Checklist

_____ When you and your family move to another community, look for a church home immediately and expectantly. Move your membership along with your furniture.

_____ When you look for a church to join, give it a real try. Be more than a taster. It won't be a carbon copy of the church you left, but there may be some wonderful new spiritual adventures in store.

_____ If your name is on a membership record, let the church, and the minister, minister to you. If you do not want that, and do not want to support it in any way, ask that your name be dropped.

_____ If you think there are things wrong in your church, help to make them right.

_____ Withhold judgments and opinions about the church, the pastor, and the people until you get to know them. The church is a hospital for people who are spiritually "sick" and admit to the need for spiritual healing. Can you do the same?

_____ Be honest and on the level when seeking the services of a church or minister. He will be more than glad to be of service, and you won't have to carry around unneeded guilt.

_____ Your pastor often asks forgiveness of members of his flock: for an oversight; for not checking out immediately someone's absence from worship; for the thoughtless actions of members who cause hurt to others, and which do not involve him. Is this his *job* and your *option*? Do you need to ask for forgiveness for a complaining spirit against him, for being absent without *good* reason, or thoughtlessness to him or his family?

_____ Are you a church-nomad, yes-man, user, taker, you-oughter, blamer, criticizer, thrill-seeker, ignorer, debunker, why-don't-they-er, why-do-they-er, stay-at-homer, or any combination of these?

_____ If you feel empty, rootless, spiritually un-

dernourished, you may be overfed, overwatered, overseeking. You need a balanced, steady diet. Your church can give it to you.

10
Questions about
HIS LORD

We are in the midst of one of the most exciting religious phenomena since the Day of Pentecost. We are being enveloped by a spontaneous spiritual combustion chamber, which defies all artificially organized structure and unites believers of nearly every diverse religious background.

A generation ago, *men* tried to bring this about with dreams of a superchurch. They theorized in their ivory towers, wondering why they failed. What they left out was the supreme catalyst—the Holy Spirit of God. After letting men muddle myopically about for a time, he called a halt and released his power to reverberate around the globe; and the world is beginning to "know we are Christians by our love."

Now, what are we going to do about it? We have several choices. We can become ecstatic and excited as we demonstrate love to others who also share our experience. Together we can swirl about in the pools and eddies of this happening and float happily as we hang onto the feeling—our support.

Or, joyfully, we can harness this tremendous energy and channel it to the hungry spiritual needs of others who have no purpose or direction for their lives. Now is a time to let go of the lethargic log of spiritual self-indulgence, and swim vigorously in his power—to higher ground. Now we have God's momentum.

The Church of Christ, after two thousand years, looks forward to the imminent return of Christ. What if it does not happen for another two thousand years? It is time to rethink our traditional ideas and past performance as pastors and lay people and decide whether such continued action and style will suffice. I think not. There must be new understanding and aggressive interaction in relationships between the two polarities, so that, instead of waiting it out together, we work it out. Some of the many possibilities have been discussed in the preceding chapters. One is that *all* are ministers.

"What? Me a minister? I'm not ordained. I can't speak in public. I'd be scared to death to pray out loud. How could I marry a couple? Or bury someone?" Ah, but if you are a Christian—if you profess Christ as your Savior and master of your life, you are a minister! The above religious "duties" are but one one-thousandth of what a pastor does, not what a minister is.

"Pastor, Mrs. Jones—my neighbor is sick. I have a little devotional book that might help her. Here, would you please take it over to her?" Unbelievable as this may seem, it happened. A lay Christian, a church member, believed it was the pastor's responsibility to take the book to this lady's next-door neighbor. The fact that "the Holy Spirit who is here to remind us what Christ told us to do," (John 14:26) made the visit to her sick neighbor imperative—bearing book, love, friendship, comfort, and something nourishing to eat.

Yet millions of church members expect their ministers to do their ministering for them. It is a physical impossibility for a pastor to take care of all ministries for everybody in his congregation (and others of the community who call on him) and to do their evangelizing for them. They are expected to do secretarial work, mimeographing, paint, dust pews, attend church socials, visit Sunday school classes, and have enough time for quiet and privacy to prepare themselves for preaching effectively.

Let's look into the Hebrew and Greek meanings of both Old and New Testaments, into words—translated into roles—which have become *diff*used and *conf*used. The word preacher in Hebrew is *koheleth* and means an "assembler" or "lecturer." In the New Testament, Paul states, "I was appointed a preacher and apostle." (1 Tim. 2:7 RSV) The New Testament Greek meaning parallels that of the Old: "to herald, preach, proclaim, publish." Therefore, the word "preacher," by definition, would be relegated to a special group of believers—those with the ability to preach. Those not afraid to stand up before a group and proclaim.

The word "pastor" is used sparingly—only eight times in the Old Testament (all in the Book of Jeremiah) and once in the New (AV). The meanings are the same in the Greek and Hebrew: "to tend a flock, to rule, to associate with as a friend, keep company with, a shepherd, or pastor."

Your spiritual leader, commonly referred to as minister, should be but the tender of the flock. Jesus referred to himself as the Good Shepherd.

In Jer. 3:15, the word acquires its metaphorical usage. After the northern and southern kingdoms were divided, God spoke through Jeremiah, disappointed and angry at the behavior of his once great people. To Israel, who has shown herself less faithless than Judah, he pleads with his children to return to him again: "And I will give you pastors [shepherds] according to mine heart, which shall feed you with knowledge and understanding." Obviously he is not speaking to four-legged sheep, but to a broken people, whose corrupt priests and bloody sacrifices had become meaningless. They needed "pastors according to my heart," full of compassion.

Shepherds have special abilities—to guide, not goad; to

nudge, not push; to move sheep together, not drive them apart—to a place of overflowing abundance. To let them lie down in green pastures when in need of rest, and drink from still, not troubled, waters. But it is the sheep, not the shepherds, who produce new lambs! Pastor-shepherds must guide the sheep (believers) to produce the new lambs for the flock.

The word "minister" has an entirely different meaning. In Hebrew, "sharath" means "to attend, as menial, or worshipper, to contribute to, minister unto, to serve, wait on." "Minister" (and, as above, derivations such as ministering, ministrations) in the Greek is also related solidly to the meaning of the Old Testament: "A worker for the people, to perform religious or charitable functions, functionary in the Temple or Gospel, worshipper of God, or benefactor of man, wait upon as a host, friend, or teacher, minister unto, to run on errands, a waiter in menial duties, could be a teacher, pastor, deacon, minister, or servant." The root word in Greek is *diaconeo*, from which the New Testament extracted the word diaconate, or deacon. From all these shades of meaning, *not one person who professes to claim Christ as Savior can claim immunity from being a minister.* Because everyone can serve!

Our Lord himself set the supreme example: He walked miles to heal and to teach, became dirty, hungry, and tired. He washed the sweaty feet of his disciples—a hospitality custom of his day, and a task that none of the twelve offered to do. He ministered to little children, nuisances to the adults. He helped out an embarrassed host at a wedding, and made a little man up in a tree feel mighty big.

He masterfully wove the menial, the mundane, into his teachings, giving his cloak, carrying a weary traveler's gear, sharing food, caring for wildlife, and patching an old garment.

His was the role of the menial, the suffering, and the sacrificial servant.

This is the example he set: *Ministering is not for pastors only.* His death brought about the "priest-hood"—the "minister-hood" of all believers.

Are you a Christian? You are a minister. Are you a Christian salesman? You are a minister. Are you a Christian engineer? You are a minister. Are you a Christian mother or father? You are a minister. Are you a Christian artist, singer, or writer? You are a minister. Are you a Christian teacher? You are a minister with an awesome responsibility to your students. Are you (whatever it may be), and a Christian? You are a minister. It does not take a special ability to wait upon, to serve someone in need; run errands for those who cannot do so; be a friend; or cook a meal for someone who is ill; or look in on someone who is lonely. In doing any of these, you are Christ's minister, doing for others what Christ himself would do if he were here. You would be building up the Body of Christ, and opening the door for those outside the Body of Christ, because you cared. You ministered.

It's so beautifully clear, and so simple. Maybe that's why most Christians miss it completely. This concept was so clearly brought home some years ago when my husband and I were on a preaching mission in Scandinavia. During our few days in the charming little city of Boras, Sweden, we were guests in the home of a successful Swedish businessman. We "conversed," with the aid of some English from our host, a bit of Swedish from us, and exaggerated gestures. My husband asked our host what his business was.

In a thick accent, this personable, warm man answered, "I'm a Christian, sir."

Thinking that he had not understood the question, my husband asked again, "But sir, I did not ask what church you attended, or your faith, I asked what is your business, your career?"

The man looked unwaveringly at him and replied, courteously but firmly, "I'm a Christian, sir. I sell Ford automobiles to pay the bills."

This Swedish businessman had found the key to his ministry without equivocation. We later learned that all the while he was selling cars, he was "selling," with sensitivity, the love of Christ to his customers.

Webster defines minister: a "servant or attendant" as archaic. This shows how far removed today's interpretation is from the original meaning of the word to the early Christians. The concept of one man ministering to the needs and demands of a group of people, large or small, namely a group of Christian believers, and doing their ministering for them, is totally incompatible with first-century ministering. It is a sad distortion, which has rendered the twentieth-century church almost impotent. As far back as Isaiah, the prophet told about the Suffering Servant. (Isa. 53 AV)

Jesus said, "Even as the Son of man came not to be ministered unto, but to minister, and to give his life a ransom for many." (Matt. 20:28 AV) Our Lord refused to be ministered *to!* After all, in the eyes of the vast majority of both Jews and Romans, he was a poor Palestinian carpenter from Nazareth—what good could come from there? Jesus was emphatic about what it meant to minister when he told an overly ambitious mother, who wanted her sons to be honored, "Whosoever will be great among you let him be the minister." (Matt. 20:26 AV) Many of the newer translations use the synonym "servant," and "slave" for minister. Can you imagine what would happen in our highly competitive age if Christians took this injunction seriously? We'd turn the world upside down again!

A closer look at the Gospels turns up some other interesting things about ministering: that it is not the property of our Savior, his disciples, the priest, or the pastor. "And when Jesus was come into Peter's house, he saw his wife's mother laid, and sick of fever. And he touched her hand, and the fever left her; and she arose, and ministered unto them." (Matt. 8:14, 15 AV) "There were also women looking on afar off; among whom was Mary Magdalene and Mary the mother of Jesus. . . . Who also, when he was in Galilee, followed him, and ministered unto him. . . ." (Mark 15:40, 41 AV)

Paul admonishes believers to minister. "For God is not unrighteous to forget your work and labor of love, which ye have shewed toward his name, in that ye have ministered to the saints, and do minister." (Heb. 6:10) "Yet I supposed it necessary to send to you Epaphroditus, my brother . . . he that ministered to my wants." (Phil 2:25 AV) But Paul was not exempt from ministering along with all believers, "I was made a minister, according to the gift of the grace of God." (Eph. 3:7 AV) He applied the idea of ministering to the mundane necessities of living, referring to his own example: "Yea, ye yourselves know, that these hands have ministered unto my necessities, and to them that were with me." (Acts 20:34 AV)

Paul called the giving of money one form of ministering. "But now I go unto Jerusalem to minister unto the saints. . . . For it hath pleased them of Macedonia and Achaia to make a certain contribution for the poor saints which are at Jerusalem. . . . For if the Gentiles have been made partakers of their spiritual things, their duty is also to minister unto them in carnal things.", i.e., material need. The church of Macedonia was in deep financial trouble, yet in their "affliction" they dedicated themselves and their means to minister to Paul, his associates and fellow saints. "Now my brothers, we must tell you about the grace that God has given to the [Greek] Macedonian churches. Somehow, in most difficult circumstances, their joy and the fact of being down to their last penny themselves, produced a magnificent concern for other people . . . they made a complete dedication of themselves first to the Lord and then to us, as God's appointed ministers." (2 Cor. 8:1, 2, 3, 5 PT)

Paul was one of God's ministers because he was one believer, but he was mainly a preacher. That was his driving motivation. He felt that other responsibilities could and should be carried on by lay believers. So he left them in the care of lay people to carry on while he went off to preach the Good News and tell about his indomitable faith. As he left Ephesus he instructed the lay-preacher substitutes "to feed and shepherd God's flock. . . . for the Holy Spirit is holding you responsible as overseers." (Acts 20:28 LB)

In fact, he wasn't at all happy with routine duties of the church. When the commissioned twelve met in the Jerusalem church, they had a good old-fashioned, outspoken church business meeting. These men complained that they were having to do everything but what Christ called them out to do. (How many pastors can empathize with that?) "We should spend our time preaching, not administering a feeding program." They instructed the lay people to "select seven men, wise and full of the Holy Spirit, who are well thought of by every one; and we will put them in charge of this business. Then we can spend our time in prayer, preaching, and teaching." (Acts 6:1-4 LB) The pastor's three primary responsibilities—then. What about today?

If Paul were to address an Epistle to the Christian church, U.S.A., now, I wonder what he would say. Would he commend it or condemn it? No doubt he would be happy to see the beginnings of a new early church kind of vitality. I believe he would be overjoyed about the renewed work of the Holy Spirit crossing all denominational barriers—not by superorganization, but by superspontaneity.

But how would he respond to the lack of response of the vast majority of church members who "joined" a church, never to minister, always to be ministered to. How much praise and patience would he have with the church, which has pushed his priorities of praying, preaching, and teaching into the background to be replaced by duties and pressures which could be attended to by a ministering church and competently trained assistants and lay people.

What are the primary priorities of Paul and his early preachers being exchanged for? To name a fractional few:

Administrator of all church activities, meetings, Sunday school, church dinners, women's meetings, laymen's programs, Boy Scouts, etc.

Counselor for marriages to be, for marriages breaking up, parents, teen-agers, and other personal problems of members of his parish, and others.

Receptionist for dozens of phone calls daily, mail, requests from people who walk in off the street, salespeople, in addition to a secretary's heavy demands in these areas, if he's lucky enough to have one.

Custodian in thousands of smaller churches, where there is no money to hire help.

Complaint Department Manager for conflicting meeting dates, meeting rooms, calls not made, hurt feelings, dropouts of duties earlier assumed, and so forth.

Moderator of church business meetings, preparing agenda for congregational business meetings, which usually require more patience than a Job could muster.

Attender of all church meetings.

Officiator of weddings and funerals, having to switch gears quickly from one to the other.

Writer of ten to one hundred letters a week, church bulletins, and several "good, uplifting, and helpful" sermons, and Bible studies weekly.

Invocationer at community and church luncheons and banquets.

Lecturer for service clubs, commencements, award dinners, etc., to keep in touch with the world outside the church.

Visitor to the sick and troubled (every pastor wishes he had more time for these). To people whose feelings are hurt and who feel neglected.

Enlister (perhaps more accurately "goader"), pushing, pulling, tugging, pleading for lay people to help in the ministries of the total church work.

Socializer at social functions, class parties, teas, receptions, and other kinds of gatherings, always being careful not to overlook saying hello to someone, who might feel it was intentional.

Because life is so different now, it is unrealistic to compare Paul's kind of pastoring with that needed today. But the pastor is not to be a glorified errand boy. The most important priorities should be at the top, not the bottom, of the list. With the help of a ministering church, it would be possible.

If, after giving some thought to it, you are convinced there is nothing you can do, and that ministering is strictly the pastor's job, there is something seriously wrong. The church's ministry is *your* ministry! If one member of the Body is not functioning the whole Body is malfunctioning.

Though ordinarily you think your toenail is an insignificant part of your body, should it become infected and cause pain it suddenly becomes mighty significant. Because it is not functioning properly you can think of nothing else.

In the Body of Christ you may feel no more important than that toenail. But by not functioning, you cause pain and distress to the whole Body. You may be that one member-of-the-Body that can make it ineffective!

The overriding concern of pastors is for Christians in their fellowship who are not growing. These Christians are like a retarded person, with a physically developed body housing the mind of a child. Tragically, the church is full of them! They believe they are "adult" Christians because they have been in the church for years.

They are like the little boy, who, after ten kisses, four prayers, and six drinks of water finally settled down for the night. As his parents breathed a sigh of relief, they heard a loud thud from his bedroom. They dashed back to find out what had happened.

"Don't know, Daddy," he rubbed his eyes. "Guess I got too close to where I got in!" An overwhelming many "stayed too close to where they got in."

> The primary responsibility for God's ministry in the world is the responsibility of the laity and not the clergy. While this may seem so simple to the seminarian or pastor, it is foreign to the ears of many a church member. The common attitude is that the clergy are paid to do the visiting, the evangelism, the social programs—in short to do all that Christ commanded each of *us* to do. This "religion by proxy" attitude must be eliminated for renewal to take place. When the fellow sitting in the pew begins to bear some of the burden for the work of the church, then renewal can begin.[1]

143

I have a beautiful rose garden. Its beautiful, colorful, fragrant flowers give me endless delight. But occasionally I observe a particular bush with special interest. Many of the flowers are developing as they should, while one of the buds stays behind. It is perfectly formed. It has had the same nutrients and care as the roses around it. I talk to it; I sing to it (at the advice of rose psychologists), but it won't flower. I wait for it and I mother it, but nothing happens. Finally I do something drastic. I cut it before it has bloomed! Still nothing!

No curling back of petals, no brilliant color; worst of all, no lovely fragrance. For a short while it remains a perfectly shaped bud, locking within all the potential of what a rose ought to be. But not for long. It withers, then it dies. It did not ever experience its beautiful potential. Its purpose was to grow, to bloom, to release its fragrance and give beauty to all who came near it. It did not consummate that ultimate purpose!

This is what is happening to countless numbers of Christians, who have the potential and purpose of the rose. To grow, to bloom, to release their fragrance and give beauty to all who come near them. What frustrates that purpose?

A lawyer, "an expert on Moses' laws came to test Jesus' orthodoxy by asking him this question: 'Teacher, what does a man need to do to live forever in heaven?' " (Luke 10:25 LB) He was not interested in spiritual truths or in the life hereafter. He was interested in trapping Jesus in theological debate.

But Jesus was ready for him. He replied, "What does Moses' law say about it?" (Luke 10:26 LB) The lawyer answered patronizingly. (He knew the law!) "It says . . . that you must love the Lord your God with all your heart, and with all your soul, and with all your strength, and with all your mind. And you must love your neighbor just as much as you love yourself." (Luke 10:27 LB) "Right," Jesus told him. "Do this and you shall live!" (Luke 10:28 LB) The man wanted to justify [his lack of love for some kinds of people], so he asked, "Which neighbors?" (Luke 10:29 LB)

To this arrogant man Jesus gave that inestimably rich parable of the Good Samaritan. It was not a member of the clergy, not a religious leader, but a *layman* who ministered to a down-and-out itinerant. He saw what needed to be done at that moment *and he did it!* He ministered.

Is it possible to love the Lord with all your heart, with all your soul, with all your strength and with all your mind? If, for one moment we become completely "one" with God, that is how much we love him. And, in that "oneness," we love our neighbor as we love ourselves. That is when we *must* minister! That is ministering!

Checklist

_____ It would be safe to say that at some time or other every pastor becomes oppressed by such thoughts as these: You're wasting your time. Sixty to eighty hours a week. What's it all for? Nothing seems to be happening. No one seems to care about their spiritual growth or that of others. And I can't do it all alone!

A ministering church is not one person ministering to a congregation. A ministering church is every member of a congregation ministering to one person. Right now, who is that one person who needs *your* ministry?

"Even the Son of Man came not to be ministered unto; but to minister!" (Mark 10:45 AV)

Test Your P.R.A.Q.
(Pastor's Responsibility
Awareness Quiz)

The following are some of the demands upon your pastor's time for a normal month. Please indicate the number of hours per week that you think your pastor should devote to these activities. Break down the hour into smaller segments if you feel it necessary. Commuting from place to place should be taken into consideration.

No. of Hours
Per Week

_____ Studying for personal, spiritual, and intellectual growth.

_____ Preparing sermons: two for Sunday and a sermon or Bible study during the week.

_____ Preparing Sunday morning worship services; including selecting Scripture, hymns; preparing for prayers, order of worship; etc.

_____ Preparing new members for baptism and church membership.

_____ Working with church school leaders.

_____ Visiting inactive members.

_____ Visiting the sick in hospitals scattered throughout the community, and in their homes.

_____ Visiting the aged and shut-ins.

_____ Evangelistic visitation on prospective new members.

_____ Visiting the bereaved at the time of tragedy or death.

_____ Visiting the bereaved sometime after the death.

_____ Visiting active families of the church.

_____ Counseling church members with practical and emotional problems.

_____ Counseling individuals and families outside the church who ask for help.

_____ Visiting time spent to soothe "hurt feelings" and members involved in relating to each other.

_____ Attending church committees and board meetings.

_____ Attending church social functions, class parties, women's meetings, etc.

_____ Staff meetings with youth minister, music director, executive lay leaders, etc.

_____ Accepting invitations for crusades and speaking engagements in other churches.

_____ Helping in community religious services: Good Friday, Thanksgiving, evangelistic crusades, religious training crusades.

_____ Counseling couples for marriage.

_____ Conducting weddings.

_____ Conducting funerals.

_____ Giving leadership in denominational activities: local, regional, and national.

_____ Speaking at service clubs, commencements, PTA, and other civic organizations.

_____ Serving on boards and committees of church-related institutions such as colleges, seminaries, and youth camps.

_____ Attending inspirational ministerial conferences and retreats to *receive* inspiration for giving out.

_____ Directing the administration of the entire church program.

_____ Promoting the entire church program.

_____ Directing the financial undergirding of the church program, including seeing to it that the church meets its budget.

_____ Writing letters and correspondence in behalf of the church.

_____ Writing personal letters to encourage the sick and discouraged.

_____ Answering and returning telephone calls.

_____ Checking on the work of church boards and committees and aiding them.

_____ Planning and helping to organize special church projects, such as Bible conferences, Christmas programs, and other special programs.

_____ Sending personal birthday cards to all members.

_____ Enlisting lay help to teach and serve in various church tasks.

_____ Working with the nominating committee to secure committee chairmen, members, and replacements for various reasons.

_____ Writing articles for the church weekly paper.

_____ Writing articles for denominational and community publications when asked to do so.

_____ Reading books and periodicals to keep up with current events, and with the latest developments in church and theological affairs.

_____ Writing to young people in college and in the services.

_____ Aiding church vacation school.

_____ Working in summer camps or adult retreats.

_____ Participating in Ministerial Association and in ministers' breakfasts.

_____ Attending and leading small group ministries.

_____ How much time for sleep and rest?

_____ How much time with his children for school programs, their fun, and their social events?

_____ How much personal time off for himself and with his wife?

_____ TOTAL (One week is 168 hours)

Please answer the following questions:

I feel the pastor should be on call twenty-four hours a day, seven days a week. (Yes_____No_____)

Should I feel free to call on the pastor at any hour of the day or night in case of extreme emergency? (Yes_____No_____)

I feel a pastor should take time off regularly. (Yes_____No_____) How much? _____

As a regularly employed lay person I have_____days off per week. Total days per year apart from vacation_____. I have_____vacation time.

How many days off should my pastor have per week?_____

How much vacation time?_____

How did you come out on this quiz? If the hours did not "balance out" for you, you are in the company of most church lay people. They made erasures, wrote over lines, and were frustrated in general. Perhaps it was best summed up by a woman who scrawled across a whole page, "This is quite an eye-opener. It can't be done!"

THEY CRY, TOO!

One layman, after laboriously struggling for a long time, finally handed in his questionnaire with the note, "Pastor, what can *I* do to help?"

That man found his ministry.

That man discovered how to love a minister and that they cry, too.

Notes

CHAPTER 1

1. John W. Meister, "A Comeback for 'Main Line' Religion?" From copyrighted article in *U.S. News & World Report*, February 25, 1974.
2. Concordia Seminary, "Take Time to Be Useful." Copyright by *Christianity Today*, April 15, 1973, p. 29. Reprinted by permission.

CHAPTER 2

1. From *A New Song* by Pat Boone. Copyright 1970 by Creation House, Carol Stream, Ill. Used with permission.
2. John C. Harris, "The Promise of Planned Self-Appraisal." Copyright 1973 Christian Century Foundation. Reprinted by permission from the January 1973 issue of *The Christian Ministry*, pp. 9–12.
3. Billy Graham, "Watergate," January 4, 1974, p. 13. Copyright by *Christianity Today*, 1974. Reprinted by permission.

CHAPTER 3

1. Stuart P. Benson, "The Making and Breaking of Pastors and Churches" appeared originally in *The American Baptist*, October 1972, p. 6.
2. Norman R. DePuy, "What's Wrong With Ministers?" appeared originally in *The American Baptist*, July–August 1973, pp. 44, 45.

CHAPTER 4

1. Constant H. Jacquet, Jr., ed., *Yearbook of American Churches*, 1972. Nashville and New York, Abingdon Press, 1972, p. 259.
2. Attributed to Harry S Truman.
3. Personal letter.

Notes

CHAPTER 5

1. Cliff Stabler, "The Care and Feeding of Shepherds." Copyright by *Christianity Today*, April 27, 1973, pp. 14, 15. Reprinted by permission.
2. *Webster's New Collegiate Dictionary* (Springfield, Mass.: G. & C. Merriam Co., 1956).
3. *Ibid.*

CHAPTER 6

1. Benson, "Making and Breaking," p. 6.
2. Dixie Sommers, "Occupational Ranking for Men and Women by Earnings," *Monthly Labor Review* (Washington, D.C.: U.S. Department of Labor, Bureau of Labor Statistics, August 1974).
3. "Supporting an Effective Ministry." (A study financed by Ministers Life and Casualty Union, in consultation with Program Committee for Professional Church Leadership of the National Council of Churches in the U.S.A.)
4. *Ibid.*
5. Jacquet, *Yearbook of American Churches*, p. 248.

CHAPTER 7

1. "Is Your Minister's Wife Expected to Be an 'Assistant Pastor'?" Advertisement, printed with permission of Ministers Life, Minneapolis, Minnesota 55416.
2. "Making Your Marriage Secure," taken from a sermon by John Rodgers.
3. *The Yearbook of American and Canadian Churches*, Nashville and New York, Abingdon Press, 1974. Figures estimated from a total of 120 million Catholic and Protestant church members.

CHAPTER 9

1. Harris, "Promise of Self-Appraisal," pp. 9–12.
2. Hugh Sidey, "The Presidency," *Life,* February 7, 1969.

CHAPTER 10

1. Findley B. Edge, *The Greening of the Church*, 1971, p. 39. Used by permission of Word Books Publisher, Waco, Texas.